THE
FOUR
ELEMENTS

FINDING RIGHT LIVELIHOOD
IN THE 21ST CENTURY

D1502542

This book is dedicated to Professor Alfred Geier,
to Roshi Robert Kennedy, and to their lifelong love
of the unknown.

CONTENTS

ACKNOWLEDGEMENTS

Many people make vital contributions to books that bear the name of only one person on the cover. I would like to thank all of my colleagues at Career and Professional Development at the Harvard Business School for their ongoing friendship and support, and for their thoughtfulness in our discussions of the ideas upon which this book is based. The coaches at Harvard have embraced this work and made it better through their use of it and the discussions that followed. I want to single out, in particular, three deeply talented leaders at the Harvard Business School: Kristen Fitzpatrick, Managing Director of Career and Professional Development; Jana Kierstead, Executive Director of the MBA and Doctoral Programs; and Lauren Murphy, former Director of Career Education and Coaching. All have been colleagues, friends, and supporters of my work for so many years. Several people took the time to read drafts of this book, I would like to acknowledge Doug Lester in particular for his time and insightful comments. Dr. Robert Parker has been an intrepid guide through Eugene Gendlin's A Process Model and my work on this project is indebted to the ideas of Professor Gendlin. Brooks Becker did a careful copy editing of this text. I would like to thank Gudrun Jobst for bringing her artistic talent and attention to detail in creating the design of this book and the accompanying website. A very special thanks to Sophie Jensen along with my best wishes for all of her adventures ahead. As always, I want to thank Linda for her patience, intelligence, wisdom, and love.

NOTES FOR THE READER

This book contains the personal stories of people with whom I have worked during their times of major life and career decision-making. Details of their identities and the specifics of their circumstances have been altered to protect their anonymity and confidentiality.

Each chapter of this book contains exercises for going deeper into the assessment of each of the Four Elements as they are operating now in your life. All of the directions necessary to participate in these exercises are contained in the chapters themselves. Additionally, you may choose to have me guide you through the exercises by listening to the podcast given for each at www.fourelementsbook.com. This feature will be available for as long as the attending website is maintained, but may be discontinued as future circumstances dictate.

THINKING FOR MEANING

Sophie Jensen was born in Copenhagen and moved with her parents to Seattle when she was five years old. Both of her parents were educators, her father a high school history teacher and her mother a special needs counselor in a suburban school district. Encouraged by her parents, Sophie was a strong student through high school and a stand-out athlete on the track team. She grew to love the outdoors through trail running with her dad in the Cascade mountains and camping on remote Washington and Oregon beaches.

Always a top performer in math, Sophie chose a computer science major but felt strongly about mixing this focus with a liberal arts curriculum at the University of Chicago. She did well in her major but was even more excited about her courses in political science, economics, and law. At graduation, Sophie accepted an offer from a growing enterprise software company working on artificial intelligence applications for clients in the financial services industry. Her company sponsored her return to a one-year master's degree program that brought her artificial intelligence skills to cutting-edge capability. On the surface, her career path seemed clear and ascendant with a strong direction in a rapidly growing industry. There was, however, a deeper story.

Sophie's most inspiring college professor taught public interest law. During her senior year, she accompanied her professor to Geneva for an international conference on human rights law. Sophie's experience there as a small group discussion facilitator was a highlight of her undergraduate experience. She kept in close touch with her friends who had been similarly inspired and had chosen law school at graduation. Two of these friends were now developing careers in Immigration Law, an interest that Sophie shared with a passion. Sophie read extensively in this area and was always eager to hear about her friends' latest projects. She closely followed the work of major organizations involved in human rights work, particularly the UN. The time came when she could no longer ignore the tension between her current work, exciting as it was in a number of ways, and her growing pull toward working on immigrant issues. Where did she truly belong? At the time she sought me out, she had been back at her company for one year following the completion of her graduate degree.

There were other important forces at play in her current situation. It was now clear that her relationship with Javier, who had recently finished business school, was serious. Javier had a plan. His extended family owned several businesses in Mexico City, where he was born and raised. After two years of deliberation, he now felt that his future lay in his home country and with the family enterprise. Sophie realized that this was a matter of heart for him, but the implications for her were profound. The move to a new country just at the time when she was considering a major career change seemed overwhelming. She found herself simultaneously at three frontiers: committing to a relationship with Javier, entering law school at age thirty, and moving to Mexico.

Sophie's first phone session with me began the way many do. Her energy and rapid speech spoke of a sense of excitement bordering on urgency. There was a lot going on in her life that she needed to sort out as major decisions were looming. Many things were happening and happening at the same time. The stakes seemed very high. In the face of all of this she was doing what we all do, trying to pick up each issue of her life situation, one at a time, and think it through to a place of resolution. The problem, of course, was that again and again she would realize that any shift in her thinking and feeling about one issue would change her view on the other pressing issues. They were all connected, all part of this very complex reality of her life as a living and breathing whole. How could she pick up the issues together and think and feel about all of them simultaneously? Despite her education at some of the finest schools in the world, she had no notion as to how this could be done.

When, like Sophie, we are at times of life impasse, it may seem as if we are being overwhelmed by a highly charged inner conversation. There are different voices, each laying a claim on our current reality, that are pressing to be heard. At one moment, one seems to have the upper hand and at another moment, another. There is the voice that speaks for adventure and a change in scenery. There is a voice that is anxiously focused on maintaining a sense of security. There is a voice that seeks elaboration and expression of our individuality, which contrasts with a very social voice that seeks to remain connected to a familiar and comforting social world. There are others as well, each with its own implicit assumptions about fulfillment and happiness, each laying its claim to what we should be doing and how and where we should be working and living. When we come to a moment in life where a deep instinct for change is aroused, this very instinct seems to awaken an inner chorus.

All of us have been where Sophie was when she first came to see me. At these times, we are facing what I call *decisions that require the full self.* Such decisions require a deep listening to all of the voices that are present. These decisions require ways of thinking that are substantially different from our usual modes of problem-solving. Analytical thinking is a powerful human capacity but it will not allow us to arrive at *meaning*. For over forty years now, I have worked with individuals facing times of major life transition. In this book, I want to share what I have learned about the *type* of thinking that we need at these crossroads, and to share, as well, what we need to be thinking *about*.

Much of my research has involved big-data type analyses of

psychological assessments to understand how people will best find their way to the work and the working environments that will be most rewarding for them. Over the past seven years, however, I've been asking a different question: After forty years of research inquiry and counseling experience, what have I learned about the issues that are *always present* when we face major life decisions? To answer this, I have looked back over my clinical experience with thousands of individuals at all stages of the life cycle in an attempt to identify the key life elements that are always present and in need of attention if we are to find our way forward. From this work I derived a model of Four Elements that form an archetypal base for our working life as well as our life broadly speaking. These elements are indeed always present, whether we are aware of them or not, and each must be engaged in turn at times of significant life decision-making: *Identity, Community, Necessity, and Horizon.*

THE FOUR ELEMENTS

The first element, *Identity*, encompasses the human need to be identified as an individual, to emerge as someone who has recognizable talents, interests, and intentions. This recognition is both inward, as a deep sense of who we are, and outward as we become more and more recognized as a person who is *like this*. These talents, interests, and intentions form a vector, a direction that is sometimes, but not necessarily, called a "career." This sense of who we are and what we can do, if developed over time, allows us to be recognized and honored for our uniqueness. It also allows others to think of us when an organization has a job to be done and is in search of the right person to do it.

Nothing is automatic about the building of identity. It is not something that is given to us and, unlike physical growth, it is not spontaneous. It has to be accomplished. It is a human task that has many facets. The efforts required to forge identity are characterized by crises, missteps, changes in direction, and the development of the will and courage to say yes to some paths and no to many. The road to identity never travels a straight line. It is not about a "sameness" that endures over time in an otherwise constantly changing world, but rather an ever-growing sense of confidence in what we need to do next, in the midst of that constant change. In the world of work, the key aspects of identity include skill and role, referring to what value we add to our place of work and what we actually do on a day-to-day basis.

The second element, *Community*, arises from the human need to feel more and more at home. It is about finding a place that is right for us. This "place" is constituted on many dimensions: family of origin, life partner, immediate family, circle of friends, religious and social organizations, immediate geographical place, connection with the immediate natural world, and nation. In the world of work, community manifests as *organizational culture* (at all of its levels: industry, company, work team, and relationship with boss). Over time, we discover which organizational cultures will allow us to thrive and which will not. It is a lesson that we often, at least early in our work life, learn the hard way.

The third element, *Necessity*, is inseparable from the reality of work. There is something in work, as exciting and rewarding as it may at times be, that is experienced as hard, aversive, and even, when conditions are harsh, as affliction. "That's why they call it work," as the saying goes. The Book of Genesis reminds us that humankind lives "East of Eden" and that work is part of our condition, is part of the very definition of what is necessary to be human. Food must be raised or bought and the rent must be paid, along with the tuition and healthcare bills. A big part of the *meaning* of our work is found in the fact that it allows us to take care of what is necessary for ourselves and those we love.

The career advice to "follow your passion" has been in vogue for many years now, but passion can only be lived out within the gravitational field of necessity.

Our final element is *Horizon*. This is the element of ultimate concern. What have we been walking *toward*? What are our work and life choices all about and for? What does our work bring into the world and how does it feed our being? These questions are not the prerogative of those of us who are explicitly religious. As much as necessity itself, they are part of our being human. The route question of Horizon is, "How do I understand and move closer to life in its fullest?"

Identity, Community, Necessity, Horizon; just the naming of each constitutes an archetypal realm. Each word itself points to an essential field of human concern. These elements are operating implicitly every day of our lives. When we are living fully and well, we do not stop to analyze the nuances of our roles at work, the various strands of affiliation that weave together to form our community, the various demands pressing on our cash flow, or just how this particular day moves us to an ultimate sense of fulfillment. But when there is a crisis such as the loss or potential loss of a job, a seemingly inexplicable loss of energy and enthusiasm, a family crisis, or a health issue, our routines of thought and action are halted and we begin a search. Something is amiss or out of alignment, something is threatened. It is at times like these that we begin a process that, if accomplished well, must unfold with deep attention to all Four Elements. Invited or not, the next movement in our life has begun. We are about to craft the next, hopefully larger, house for our work and our lives.

These elements constitute the *what* of our thinking at the cross-roads. To this, I have added my research work on the *how* of the thinking that is required. The full-self thinking that is required for major life decisions is accomplished using non-analytical modes of human cognition. Specifically, I have taught my students and counseling clients over the years how to engage in what I refer to as *implicit intelligence* and *symbolic intelligence* when they are faced with questions of meaning and purpose.

In this book, you will pick up each of the Four Elements in turn and attempt to understand them as thoroughly as possible so that you can recognize how they are showing up right now in your current life situation. You will then be able to participate in exercises that engage your *implicit understanding* of your *whole life situation* as seen through the lens of each particular element. The next step is learning how to translate what you already know implicitly into fresh new language, *symbolic* intelligence, that you can use to find a new way forward. This book is written to be practical and to move swiftly. The psychological and philosophical underpinnings of the ideas being presented as tools will be provided in Appendix I and the References if you want to learn more about how they animate this approach. As we proceed, we will follow Sophie as she moves through her own engagement with each of the Four Elements.

IDENTITY

In the 1996 movie *Big Night*, two brothers, Primo and Secundo, come from Italy to open a restaurant. They have high hopes and are full of youthful energy, but it is not at all clear if they are artists or restaurateurs. Nearby is the restaurant run by Pascal, an older man and a savvy operator who fills his establishment every night despite an unexceptional menu. Pascal offers his help, but it turns out to be a scam to drive the brothers, his new competition, out of business. When they begin to comprehend that they have been taken, they question him, incredulously and with indignation: "Who *are* you?" Pascal's response: "I am a businessman, who are *you*?"

The hearts of the audience are, of course, with the young and attractive brothers who have become victims. But the wisdom of Pascal is not lost. He is older, wiser, and, as he states, he knows who he is. His business is successful because he has no pretensions of being a cutting-edge chef. He serves serviceable spaghetti and meatballs at a good price, and his customers come back again and again. Pascal came to an understanding a long time ago: he would take care of his family and make it in America by focusing on business results. His customers, his family, his friends know him as someone who has found what he wants to do and takes enjoyment in doing it. He has an identity, an identity that works.

But what is it exactly that Pascal has and that Primo and Secundo have yet to acquire? The predicament that the brothers find themselves in at the end of the movie begs the questions that are at the heart of this book: Who are you? What do you do? What do you want to do next? What do you need to do next? How do you find out? These are questions of the heart that follow us in life. They are questions of identity.

Identity is not the same thing as confidence. An individual with a strong sense of work identity will have up days and down days, just like everyone else. She will experience failures and setbacks and even go through periods of impasse where the way forward in work does not seem at all clear. Through these times of trial, however, she will have a deeper sense of what she is about, of what her interests and sources of inspiration are, of what her signature talents are, of what endeavors she should avoid because of skill deficits. She will have an understanding of the types of work environments that energize her and those that don't. She will be aware of the constraints, economic and otherwise, that place limits on her options. Her identity has in some way been laid down and will, during times of turbulence, lead her back to a center where she can make decisions that are authentic and move her in a direction that is expansive rather than contractive.

During times of uncertainty and crisis, which may last for many months or longer, the environment, her friends, her family, her colleagues, and her "network" will not lose or forget her identity. Something has been built that is durable or that at the very least has a "half-life" that lasts a long time. The fiction writer J.D. Salinger stopped publishing and disappeared from public view when he was a still a young man. As the decades rolled by, nonetheless he remained the "brilliant fiction writer." Even in the absence of fame, identity outlives biology amongst the social network that helped to forge it. I could tell you stories about my uncle Bill, dead for decades, that would allow you to know him as a highly differentiated person who had a particular approach to life and way of doing things.

IDENTITY FELT AND OBSERVED

Identity is an "inside" and "outside" phenomenon. On the one hand, the deeply felt enthusiasms, the enactment of signature talents, the real world demands encountered, the knowledge gained from experience, do not exist apart from the experience of a particular individual who is living them and building an identity as she does so. On the other hand, from what is known as the social constructivist perspective, there is a way in which our world constructs, contributes to, amplifies, transmits, confirms, recognizes, and records our identity. From this latter perspective, identity is not just a subjective experience, and we who live it are not its sole owners.

There is a way in which even the most elaborated application of a social constructivist view fails to capture the deeper reality of work identity. As actually lived, the creation of identity is an existential struggle. Work identity, even for the most educated and talented, is a hard-won human accomplishment that rarely unfolds in a straight line. Furthermore, self-awareness and identity are accretive: they grow as we live our lives in an ongoing process of experience, reflection, and choice. Our identity project at age nineteen is not our identity project at twenty-eight, which in turn is different from our identity projects at forty and sixty.

Identity, of course, is bigger than what we do and what we have to offer at our place of work. The project of building a self that faces and participates in the world is a life task, and our working identity is one dimension of that project. The forces that shape identity do not recognize artificial boundaries between our work world and our world writ large. If issues such as race, gender, or nationality have shaped the formation of our identity, they play their role at work as well as in our neighborhood. Our focus in this book, however, is not to try in a superficial way to come to terms with these powerful forces. Our focus is on the two tasks that, regardless of our other identity issues, lie at the heart of what we must accomplish in order to establish our place in the working world: determining what our work role will be, and determining what in the way of aptitude and talent we have to offer.

THE WORKING IDENTITY TASK

When Ravi Deshpande came to see me at the Harvard Business School, he was approaching his thirty-fifth birthday and experiencing an identity impasse. Ravi came from a high-achieving family that held high expectations for him. He attended an excellent prep school and an Ivy League college. Along the way, Ravi had decided to follow his father, a prominent gastroenterologist, into the medical profession. He was accepted into a leading medical school and afterward entered and completed an arduous six-year surgical residency at Stanford. He then became an attending surgeon in the Stanford system. But here he was, a first-year business school student who had sought me out for help with career direction.

We eventually got around to the question that would have been on everyone's mind: "Why are you here?" "I always relished the idea," he responded, "of being able to tell people at cocktail parties that I was a surgeon." He went on: "I enjoyed medical school and admire so many of my colleagues, but what I honestly now feel is that I am a low-level employee in a very large corporation." He then told me that the day-to-day realities of doing the things that surgeons do did not deeply engage his true interests. It was a pragmatic, craftsperson-like role that fell short of the high level of interpersonal interaction that he had since come to understand was so important for him.

Other than when in the operating room, he did not feel that he was "in charge" in the sense of making strategic or creative decisions that shaped the lives of those around him. He missed the world of his liberal arts undergraduate courses and his participation in team projects. He had been a leader in several clubs where he enjoyed introducing new initiatives. He found himself envying his friends from college who were now in management roles in business organizations and, as he imagined it, working in highly social environments on creative projects that were largely under their control.

Ravi's crisis turns on issues of work identity. At the heart of work identity are two important concepts: *role* and *contribution*. These ideas are closely related. Role refers to what we actually do on a day-to-day basis. For Ravi, as a surgeon, this entailed meeting with referred patients; performing the necessary review of history, test results, and physical exams to determine the appropriateness of surgery; the actual surgical operations; and patient follow-up. This is how he spent most of his waking hours. I have found in my work that role satisfaction is highly related to underlying patterns of deeply imbedded life *interests*.

Contribution, though correlated with role, is more related to our *aptitude* and developed *skills*. It is what we bring to our place of work, that particular contribution of enthusiasm, aptitude, learned skill, intelligence, knowledge, experience, and personal presence. Ravi brought his considerable general intelligence, his genuine wish to help others, an aptitude for acquiring the wide range of knowledge about the human organism required of any competent physician, the physical stamina required to take his place in a busy surgical practice, and the intricate surgical skills acquired by many years of apprenticeship and practice. Ravi, for sure, found satisfaction in some of the aspects of his surgical work but ultimately came to the conclusion that he did not want to be spending his days the way surgeons spend their days. He felt deeply, as well, that his potential to contribute as a leader of others and to direct creative organizational projects was going unfulfilled.

Perhaps the most immediate way for all of us to pick up the issue of our work identity is to ask the questions that Ravi had been asking himself in a profound way during the year in which he was making the high-stakes decision to leave the world of medicine: "What do I truly want to be doing every day?" and "What is that mixture of aptitude, skill, energy, and presence that I have to offer?" At times of impasse, when it is not clear what we are called to accomplish in the next stretch of life, we must find a way to intimately grasp, with a detailed particularity, what role we must step into, and what we have to offer in that role.

FINDING NEW LANGUAGE FOR MEANINGFUL ROLES

There is a paradox at the heart of identity. It is on one hand a durable sense of self deeply felt by us and recognized by those around us. On the other hand, our identity is continually being forged in the smithy of our lived experience. At times of crisis and transition we do not face the task of inventing a new identity, but of taking hold of how our identity will *now* be lived and grow within our changed life circumstances.

If we are living with an intention for self-awareness and fulfillment, we will become more complex, more intricate, more particular, more uniquely ourselves, as we gain experience and knowledge in our movement through life. This greater intricacy means that we cannot simply cut and paste from our last existential encounter with "what needs to come next." We need to do the work anew, the work of holding a deep felt sense of the whole of our life situation and then finding new and fresh language that will allow us to fully "have" what we find. At times of crisis, transition, and impasse, we must redraw our self-portrait in a fresh way that allows us to see the very particular features of a face that is deeply familiar, but alive and aged precisely to this moment in our life.

The redrawing, or rather rewriting, that we will now do is designed to take us from a deep implicit sense of what is emerging to a fuller symbolic knowing in the form of three carefully crafted sentences that capture what we know and bring it into the realm of fresh and actionable language. These sentences arise from what we know implicitly about who we are and what we do. To write them, we dig into what we have previously learned, and implicitly know, about who we are and what we do. These sentences, however, if we write them well, will reveal something quite new: They will reveal how our work identity needs to manifest in our now changed world.

The process will use a method based on *Thinking at the Edge*, an approach that developed out of Eugene Gendlin's Philosophy of the Implicit. It proceeds in four steps. Do not worry about where the process is going but rather take your time and focus on the direction for each step in itself. In the side box you will be able to read about the experience of Sophie Jensen, whom we met in Chapter One, as she went through this "deep dive" experience. It may be helpful for you to glance at her examples as you go along.

When the priming question is asked in Step 1 below, you must *observe* your answer rather than *think* about your answer. This can only be done from a place of "free attention": an alert, completely open field of non-attached awareness. The capacity to hold oneself in a state of free attention is a skill that must be learned and regularly practiced. It is the key to what I call *implicit intelligence*. For each of the exercises in this book, you will be guided by the text into a place of free attention. You can participate in each of these exercises either by reading through the text and following the directions, or if you visit www.fourelementsbook.com. There, I will lead you through the process for using free attention and then step you through the exercise itself.

When you are ready:

Sit in a chair with a comfortable but upright posture. Direct your attention to the middle of your torso, anywhere from your throat to your lower abdomen. Allow your free attention to rest there. Notice that keeping your attention requires an effort. As you try to do so, you become aware of the conditioned thoughts, memories, and images, and the emotions that come with them spontaneously arise. This is not your "thinking," it is mechanical, automatic. If, instead of returning your attention to the sensation in the middle of your body, you give attention to the stream of thoughts, feelings, and associations, they will become a storyline, and there will be a judgement, "This is good, this is bad, this is just neutral." You now have competition for your awareness and what you were doing with it.

Allow the emerging thoughts and emotions to follow their own course but do not feed them with your attention, with your imagination, or with your will. Do not allow images to become a string of associations that in turn become a storyline when you feed them with your attention. The trick is to see it happening and at that very point to redirect your attention to the sensation in the middle of your body. If you wish, you may return your attention to the palm of your right hand as your "foundation of mindfulness." For some people, returning their attention to the breath works best. Make a choice: center of the body, palm of the right hand, or breath, but once you make a choice stick with it.

Have no expectations as you return your attention to your foundation of mindfulness (the middle of your body, the palm of your right hand, your breath). Allow your attention to rest there, giving your attention to the bodily sensation the energy that it needs so as not to be caught up in the string of thoughts, emotions, associations, and judgements. Have an open and curious mind. Do not expect anything. Suspend the need of your analytical mind to figure out what is happening or to impose any type of order or understanding onto your experience. Suspend your need, the need of your conditioned analytical mind to know, to have a sense of where things are going, or to have a sense of whether or not this whole endeavor is worth it.

This experience of free attention will be a threat, in fact, to that part of you that needs to know, that needs to pin things down, that needs to get somewhere. Continue to get nowhere, continue not to know. Continue to return your attention to your foundation of mindfulness. Continue to allow whatever needs to arrive to arrive. At first, it may seem as if nothing is happening, and your "inner critic" will tell you that this is exactly so and that you are wasting your time. Whenever the inner critic appears, a good strategy is to simply smile. Do not allow your inner critic or your judging mind to interfere with your open awareness anchored in your foundation of mindfulness.

STEP 1. Writing from a Deeply Remembered Time of Full Engagement at Work

From the place of a concentrated returning to the middle of your body, holding an open curiosity of how things are right now, allow a memory of a time at work when you felt deeply engaged, in the "flow." Let this suggestion come into your field of attention as it is anchored in the middle of your body: Allow a memory to form of a time when you were deeply engaged in your work. A time when you were so completely in the flow of your work that you lost track of time, lost track, even, of a sense of a separate self. A time when you were completely engaged, doing the work that you were born to do. There were feelings of both competence and challenge; you felt stretched but confident you could accomplish. Do not editorialize or pick or choose. Allow a memory image to come and work from that one. You are fully engaged, in the flow. How is it now in the middle of the body? Allow a felt sense to form "a direct, bodily-felt, unclear edge" of what being in this flow is. No need for words or analysis. How is it, this deep body feel of being completely given over to your work?

Go inside, focusing on how this memory feels in the middle of your body. Stay with it, returning your attention to the feeling in the middle of the body each time you get caught up in thoughts or other distractions. Allow a felt sense, a distinct bodily-felt unclear edge, to form about what it was like when you were doing that work at that time. Stay with the felt sense, even if the sensation itself begins to change. From the felt sense, write a rough, free-flowing paragraph about what was exciting and energizing.

STEP 2. Find the Crux of the Experience and Capture It in One Sentence

From the felt sense, write a sentence that describes the crux of your paragraph, of what was so interesting about what you were doing at that time, even though the sentence is not just right. Underline or bold the **key word or phrase** in that sentence.

STEP 3. If Necessary, Replace the Key Word or Phrase of Your Sentence with the Fresh Language of a New Sentence

If the sentence that you have written wakes you up because it has fresh language that allows you to truly explain a vital aspect of what a meaningful role is for you, proceed to Step Four. If not, replace the **key word or phrase** with a whole new fresh sentence that *comes out of* the **key word or phrase** and captures the essence of your peak role experience in a more nuanced and specific fashion. In this way, your **key word or phrase** provides a new launching point for a new sentence, one that goes beyond your first, more automatic, response. Underline the **key word or phrase** of this new sentence. This sentence now captures an essential peak role "facet."

STEP 4. Allow Another Bodily-Felt Peak Role Memory to Form and Repeat the Process

Go back to Step One and allow a new memory and felt sense of that remembered experience to form. Repeat Steps Two and Three to arrive at a final sentence with fresh language; this will be your second peak role facet. Then go through the process a third time to collect a third role facet. At the end of this exercise, you will have three sentences, each bringing new language to an essential element of work activity that is inherently meaningful for you. You will have described three essential facets of your peak role experience.

SOPHIE JENSEN

Meaningful Work Roles

STEP 1. Writing from a Deeply Remembered Time of Full Engagement at Work

The core of me is solid and full. I feel deeply engaged and alive but not on-edge. I'm at the center of a small-to-medium group of recently started AI analysts. I'm facilitating a session on "creative design." I feel energized by my own energy and engagement, as well as theirs. I, we, are weaving something together out of content that is partially already there but also out of thoughts and inspiration that appear in real time. I love the new, different people; I love being at the center to help us weave something together; I love making them laugh and also think. It's important to me to try to impart to them something of what it will take to keep their own cores solid and full in the vortex that is SkyTech. I'm so "in" the moment; I'm thinking and doing from *within* that moment, rather than thinking and doing in a way that is somehow disassociated from the present moment and laced with anxiety. I am giving and creating and experimenting and teaching. I am expanding.

STEP 2. Find the Crux of the Experience and Capture It in One Sentence

I am anchored and yet I'm fluid as I **orchestrate and teach** a group of recent hires, making them **laugh and think** and, I hope, settle more into themselves.

STEP 3. If Necessary, Replace the Key Word or Phrase of Your Sentence with the Fresh Language of a New Sentence

I am anchored and yet I'm fluid, as I ~~orchestrate and teach~~ weave people and thoughts and inspiration together with a group of recent hires, making them ~~laugh and think~~ engage, enjoy, reflect, and, I hope, settle more into themselves.

STEP 4. Allow Another Bodily-Felt Peak Role Memory to Form and Repeat the Process

2nd Memory

Writing from a Deeply Remembered Time of Full Engagement at Work

I am completely engaged and yet relaxed. I'm drawing on a reservoir of knowledge and experience but also operating with high responsiveness to what's happening in real time. I'm working one-on-one with Harley and helping her learn how to troubleshoot the code she's been working on for her first project. I like that I'm working dynamically, interpersonally, and helping another person to grow, and not just grow themselves in a narrow sense but grow their own sphere of influence - i.e., I like my influence over *their* ability and influence. I am so in the moment and responding to what's arising in real time that I don't have a "storyline" track running in another part of my mind. It's me and the person and the situation and I'm on my toes but I'm able and intuitive and skilled; we make it fun and productive.

Find the Crux of the Experience and Capture It in One Sentence
I'm completely in the moment and, while drawing on knowledge and experience, there is also a high degree of **real-time intuition and responsiveness** as I work to fine-tune and **influence another's influence.**

If Necessary, Replace the Key Word or Phrase of Your Sentence with the Fresh Language of a New Sentence
I'm completely in the moment and, while drawing on knowledge and experience, there is also a high degree of ~~real-time intuition and responsiveness~~ **responding dynamically and intuitively** as I work to ~~fine-tune and influence another's influence~~ **expand and positively shape spheres of influence.**

3rd Memory

Writing from a Deeply Remembered Time of Full Engagement at Work
Different memories have floated to the surface. China workshop. Immigration article. Mark K's Talk. Geneva conference speech. The "felt sense" that seems to summon them all is a sense of being led by the gut; yes, there is a deeply conceptual, abstract thinking part of my "mind" at play, but that part is almost seeming to translate/capture/play with/explore what emerges from some entity within but "beyond" me. In those experiences, *I* am surprised by what emerges, though it is supposedly emerging from me myself. There is also an element of showing, sharing, shining that insight/gut/inspiration with others. I suppose

that's what's common: exploring, led by my gut, and sharing; being at the center to reveal/pass on something, but not something I feel I "knew" – something I feel I *learned*.

Find the Crux of the Experience and Capture It in One Sentence

Learning and discovering for myself and in ways that surprise and intrigue me, led by something intuitive, which pairs the power of my mind with something essential in my heart and gut – and sharing the insights of that with others.

If Necessary, replace the Key Word or Phrase of Your Sentence with the Fresh Language of a New Sentence

Learning and ~~discovering~~ exploring deeply for myself and in ways that surprise and intrigue me, led by something intuitive, which pairs the power of my mind with something essential in my heart and gut – and ~~sharing the insights~~ weaving together the threads and sharing that with others.

The patterns that emerge from this exercise have their origin in deeply embedded life interests. To them, you must add another set of ingredients. Our aptitudes, and the skills that develop from them, are closely related to our deep interests. Over time, we need to develop many skills to be effective in our work, but our strongest tend to be related to what interests us most and what comes to us most naturally. I refer to these as *signature skills*. They are not captured on any skills checklist such as the ability to code in Python or speak French fluently. If you want to claim your signature skills, and be able to describe them to yourself and anyone who might inquire about them, you must find the new language that will allow you to truly own them.

FINDING NEW LANGUAGE FOR YOUR SIGNATURE SKILLS

We often, and incorrectly, use the words "skill," "aptitude," and "talent" interchangeably. An aptitude is an underlying potential that might take several paths to expression as a skill. Someone with an innate athletic aptitude might, with instruction and practice, become a great basketball free-thrower. A skill is the direct exercise of an ability as when a trained carpenter makes a precise cut to fit two joints meeting at a difficult angle. Talent is a more general term that refers to an ability that exists both as a general aptitude and as varying specific skill expressions.

If we grow up in a caring environment, those who care for us begin to notice our aptitudes and mirror them to us. I remember sensing that the son of my friend, at a very early age, had a firm sense of his body in space and that his movement was unusually focused and coordinated. I was not at all surprised, years later, when he made the high school varsity basketball team as a freshman. I remember, as well, my daughter singing a little song for a colleague of mine when she was three years old. My colleague, a deep admirer of classical music, broke from his joking banter with her and turned to my wife and me saying, "She has real talent. You need to nurture her music." Music, it turned out, was the very thing around which she built her adolescent identity that allowed her a transition to young adulthood.

This pointing out to a young person something that comes naturally to her, something she has verve for, is a vital gesture. It allows something to continue hatching. It encourages her to make the effort to experience more, learn more, practice more so that aptitude can become the exercise of skill that brings a sense of competence and delight. This mirroring has an evil twin, a "near enemy" as the Buddhists say; something that sounds the same as encouragement and blessing, and is thus confusing to the child or young adult, but is really something quite different. This false mirroring does not come from careful observation of the child but rather from the narcissistic need of a parent or other adult for the child or adolescent to be seen as exceptionally talented so that the ensuing recognition redounds to the adult. When the mirroring is authentic, however, the child is affirmed that what excites them is indeed valued, worthwhile, and worthy of their continued efforts.

This mirroring, from true friends, teachers, and mentors, can continue as we grow. More and more we can become affirmed in what we have to offer the world. More and more, we can, through effort, allow what is essential aptitude to become differentiated and specific skills. When we are working from within the stream of this aptitude, we feel the energy and naturalness that arises from the flow of that stream. Even when facing uncertainty, even when we clearly do not know the answer, there is a way of approaching, a way of contending, a way of meeting our circumstances. It will always be important to learn new skills and to try things that are *not* natural, that may feel awkward, but which we are nevertheless called to master for the time being. But they, too, are taken on from the stream of what we know to be our essential effectiveness. They are part of an experimentation and as such are part of an at times effortful unfolding of what we are, rather than an attempt to be something or somebody else.

Shirley came to see me for career counseling during her first year on campus. By many measures, she had been a high achiever in the financial services firms where she had worked for four years before coming to Harvard. She was the daughter of first-generation Eastern European immigrants who had high expectations for her professional success. She was very good in math and a sharp critical thinker. She was also, I came to see as I got to know her, capable of close observation and deep reflection. She was a thoughtful observer of people and situations and was very psychologically minded. These latter qualities, however, seemed outside of her awareness. Apparently, they had not been honored and mirrored to her. In her family, in her college major chosen on her math ability, and in her career path to date in financial services, these aptitudes did not "count." Consequently, Shirley herself did not count them. She couldn't; she *had no language for them*.

After getting to know Shirley better, I reflected these qualities for her by pointing out how they manifested in our counseling sessions and by giving them names: "close observation of behavior," "thoughtful conclusions drawn from these observations," "psychological mindedness," "a natural interest in personalities and behavior." Reality does not reside in a name, but finding the right name allows it, perhaps for the first time, to be fully recognized and "owned." Shirley knew that there was something missing from her financial analyst roles; this new language allowed her imagination to move into the realm of team and general management.

In baseball, no two pitchers throw the ball in the same way. No two pitchers have the same history within the league. The savvy coach knows this and in crucial moments of critical games will swap one pitcher for another to face a particular batter. I wonder how many pitchers could tell you precisely why they are effective in some game situations but not in others. In my experience, individuals vary remarkably in their level of awareness concerning their innate talent. Many can talk about their facility with math, public speaking, or strategic thinking, but far fewer can provide a nuanced description of the very particular way they have come to be effective in employing these generic skills. I have given the name "signature skills" to these "very particular ways" that we have found to be exceptionally effective.

Finding just the right words for our signature skills is an identity-building act. Because we have made the effort to get it right, it allows us to remind ourselves in a very believable way what we indeed have to offer. It also allows us to distinguish ourselves from others who draw from the same pool of talents but use them with a different inflection and different base of life experience. The magic comes from making the effort to find just the right words. In the exercise that follows, you will be guided through a process for discovering fresh new language for the roots of three signature skills. Again, the side box will give the specific example of Sophie Jensen's experience with this process. Please refer to this example if the directions are not clear for you. We will begin, as we did for roles, from a place of free attention. Please turn now to Appendix II to be guided into a place of free attention if you want to move through the exercise by reading the text itself. Alternatively, if you visit www.fourelementsbook.com, I will lead you through the process for using free attention and then step you through the exercise itself.

STEP 1. Writing from a Deep Memory of Effectiveness at Work

At this suggestion, allow a memory to come, right away, of a situation, or repeating types of situations, where you feel you are or have been particularly effective. Just allow the memory to come without second-guessing yourself. Spontaneously write a brief paragraph that describes the type of situation where you are particularly effective.

STEP 2. Find the Crux of the Experience and Capture It in One Sentence

Write a simple sentence beginning with the phrase "My talent is . . ." that states the talent that allows you to be effective in these situations. Next, underline the **key word** in the sentence.

STEP 3. If Necessary, Replace Key Word or Phrase of Your Sentence with the Fresh Language of a New Sentence

As with the Role exercise, if the sentence that you have written wakes you up because it has fresh language that allows you to truly express the essence of your signature skill, proceed to Step Four. If not, replace the **key word** with a whole new fresh sentence that *comes out of* the **key word or phrase** and captures the essence of your talent in a more nuanced and specific fashion. In this way, your **key word or phrase** provides a new launching point for a new sentence, one that goes beyond your first, more automatic, response. Underline the **key word or phrase** of this new sentence.

STEP 4. Allow another Bodily-Felt Sense of a Signature Skill to Form and Repeat the Process

Go back to Step One and allow more images to form of something that you do particularly well. Repeat Steps Two and Three to arrive at a final sentence with fresh language; this will be your second signature skill facet. Then go through the process a third time to collect a third skill facet. At the end of this exercise, you will have three sentences, each bringing new language to an essential talent in which you have confidence. You will have described three essential signature skill facets. In the side box you will be able to read Sophie Jensen's response to this signature skills deep dive.

SOPHIE JENSEN

Signature Skills Deep Dive

Finding New Language for Your Signature Skills

STEP 1. Writing from a Deep Memory of Effectiveness at Work

I am an active coach of the junior AI analysts on my team. I approach this coaching from the perspective of seeing the person as just that: a person and not a machine. I am honest and also kind and I think they can see I am truly invested in their development. These coaching conversations often outgrow the project, and those with whom I worked continue to come to me for mentoring after the project has ended.

STEP 2. Find the Crux of the Experience and Capture It in One Sentence

My talent is **coaching** and ultimately **mentoring** young adults, **seeing** them as "360-degree" people, **caring** for their wellbeing and success and offering fresh, helpful **insights** and advice, earning their respect and trust.

STEP 3. If Necessary, Replace Key Word or Phrase of Your Sentence with the Fresh Language of a New Sentence

My talent is ~~coaching and ultimately mentoring young adults~~ growing people, ~~seeing them as "360-degree" people, caring for their wellbeing and success while~~ en-gaging with and caring for them *as* people, ~~and offering fresh, helpful insights and advice~~, expanding perspectives, earning their respect and trust.

STEP 4. Allow Another Bodily-Felt Sense of a Signature Skill to Form and Repeat the Process

2nd Memory

Writing from a Deep Memory of Effectiveness at Work
I feel conflicted about this memory because it's one where I do think I'm often very effective but it's not necessarily one where I myself always feel that comfortable or at ease. In any case, it's about facilitating group conversations, be they in-person meetings, audio/video design calls, or broader/longer workshops. I am particularly effective at structuring the conversation in a naturally flowing way, helping others feel at ease and continually weaving the threads of discussion together in a real-time synthesis of what's being said and what it means for "where next." I also do a good job of navigating conflicting opinions in a way that doesn't paper over differences but also doesn't get stuck – I seem to be quite agile in navigating us to something of a joint solution. I think I come across as calm, collected, and confident (though I often don't actually feel those things at the time).

Find the Crux of the Experience and Capture It in One Sentence
My talent is **facilitating group discussions** that put people at ease and weave together multiple perspectives into something united and whole and forward-moving.

If Necessary, Replace Key Word or Phrase of Your Sentence with the Fresh Language of a New Sentence
My talent is ~~facilitating~~ planning and orchestrating in

real-time group discussions that put people at ease and weave together multiple perspectives into something united and whole and forward-moving.

3rd Memory

Writing from a Deep Memory of Effectiveness at Work
I'm good at structuring concepts and conceptual logic and related design requirements. I can play with abstract "blocks" in my head to make sure things hang together in a logical, fluidly sequenced way that keeps the thinking, design, and discussion clear and focused. I do this most ably in my written communication, though it's reflective of how I think and probably tend to communicate verbally too. It's about placing things in the appropriate context, crystallizing the logic flow and communicating that in as clean and elegant a way as I can.

Find the Crux of the Experience and Capture It in One Sentence
My talent is **structuring thinking** and capturing it in **clean, logical, elegant written materials.**

If Necessary, Replace Key Word or Phrase of Your Sentence with the Fresh Language of a New Sentence

My talent is ~~structuring thinking~~ **creating structure out of abstract thoughts** and capturing it in ~~clean, logical, elegant written materials~~ **compelling writing**.

Renewing Your Identity Narrative

Well-written biographies will show the reader not only how the protagonist and his environment changed over the course of a lifetime but also how he became aware of these changes and how his sense of who he was changed with this new awareness. If we could use a motion picture "freeze-frame" technique and interview this protagonist at multiple times in his life, we would get different accounts of what he was doing and what he was trying to accomplish. We would see that his deep interests as a deep pattern were readily identifiable, but we would find them expressed differently in terms of activities and roles at each interview. His signature skills would also be recognizable, but we would see how they had grown and how they had been refined with life experience. Identity, like that aging face we referenced earlier, retains recognizable features but, with time, becomes something more and more unique and defined.

Our identity expression needs to change, because our circumstances and environment change. Identity does not exist independent of the other three archetypal fields in whose gravity it travels. Identity is pulled by the forces of community as roles are not abstract, but must be what our communities of the moment require. Our communities change as we take new jobs or move to new locations; they change as our families grow. Roles must bend to necessity. I lived through a period where the arrival of managed healthcare meant that many of my fellow psychologists who had worked hard to establish full-time private psychotherapy practices had to switch course and find new roles in hospitals or higher education. Many times, wisely or not, talented engineers or analysts transition to management roles to meet the financial needs of a growing family. In Chapter Six, we will see how our Horizon, too, has its pull as we look for roles where our sense of contribution is more palpable.

Signature skills become more refined and particular with work and life experience. The writer Malcom Gladwell became well known for his contention that it takes 10,000 hours for a skilled worker to claim mastery. In my observations, there is even greater refinement at 20,000 and 40,000 hours, particularly in skill areas that demand judgement, interpersonal facility, and cross-cultural experience. The question before us, particularly during times of transition or work uncertainty, is *right now*, how do we tell ourselves and others what matters the most in terms of what we want to do and what we have to offer. The poet John Ashbery said that he wrote to discover what he was thinking. Now is the time for you to pick up that task.

A TRIP TO THE MUSEUM

Place your three work role statements and three signature statements before you. Literally, have them on a page in front of you. Set aside some protected private time to read them, and to notice *how reading them affects you*. Do not try to analyze them or come to quick conclusions about how they relate one to another. Do not try to "solve them." Instead, stand before them as you would stand before a painting at a museum. At a museum, we might move quickly at first, from room to room, to get a general sense of what is available. But then we find ourselves stopped. A particular painting or sculpture will grab us, and we find ourselves in stillness before it. We do not know why this one of all the others.

As we stand in stillness, we begin to realize that the art is working on us, not vice versa. Before, we thought that we were making choices, but now we have been captured. The sculpture is showing us something that we have not yet experienced and do not yet know but that, in some way, we are pulled to experience and know. The painting is touching some part of us that is already there, but which needs to wake up. We have an implicit excitement, somewhat akin to catching the glimpse of a person across the room that we find instantly attractive or interesting, but are not sure just why. What we need to do next is to allow ourselves to be worked on. Passive voice.

Passive voice, but with great activity of attention. Not "figuring out" attention, but intently noticing attention. How are we being changed by being intently exposed to the force of what is front of us? By paying attention, we can find out, but it might be several days before we "know." It is very similar with music. The radio in the car plays and we barely notice. If quizzed, we could not come up with the songs that we "heard." But sometimes one song or an extended movement is different. It grabs us and allows us to feel something that needs to be felt. We did not know that we needed to feel these things, but we did. We needed the song, we needed the painting, we needed the sculpture.

Again, it may be days before we know what was opened up. Or, if our attention dissipates as it often does, we may never make the effort to go deeper and complete our knowing. Accomplished poets and novelists are first of all keen observers; they see and feel directly and intensely. Many of us can, at least from time to time, follow them there. But few of us take the next step, of bringing that which has been intensely experienced into language. The poets bring implicit knowing into symbolic knowing. They bring it into language so that they can fully *have* it, and, if they are very skilled, allow others to have it as well.

Reading slowly through your six sentences, allow them to work on you. Soak in them. Be curious about what is happening to you as you read. Stop and try to locate a felt sense of how they are affecting you. Keep your attention up. Be willing to not have a direction or goal. A half hour may pass with no words or conclusions. You may set the statements down because of a pressing need. If you do so, "mark" your experience by noting the body feel of how you are as you deliberately disengage. This will make it easier for you when you pick the statements up again to continue the process.

Sooner or later, you will be able to write. Write freely and spontaneously, trying to capture what is odd or different or new about your experience with the statements. What seems unusual, uncomfortable, or just stands out? What memories or associations come as you write? Fears? Excitement? Do not worry about spelling, grammar, syntax, or finely wrought phrasing. Just write. When the words stop for now, put the writing down. Return to it when you are moved to return to it. Write more or, better yet, revise what you have written, looking, this time, for just the right word or phrase, fresh language that opens up rather than defines or narrows.

What you are creating is the latest version of your work identity narrative: Your story, for now, about what work activities make you most alive and the best words, for now, that describe what you have to offer. This writing will allow you to fully *have* what you are looking for. Where to find it might not be immediately clear, but without fully knowing it, you cannot begin a true search.

When the time is right, share your narrative with your close and trusted circle. Listen to their responses to it, listen to their questions. They may help you find even better language. They may indeed have ideas about where to find the roles and offer the talents that your words portray. They may point out opportunities that are right in front of your nose but have gone unnoticed. They may suggest conversations that you should have with people at your current place of work or within their own work or social circles. They may associate to what they know or have heard about from their friends regarding other work settings.

As you are comfortable, allow the circle to widen and your story to spread. You are allowing yourself to be better seen and better known. You are inviting others into the crafting of your narrative and the effort to realize that narrative. Their circles begin to move into your circle. Their ideas provide options and action steps that had not yet come to you. If a job search or change is a stream of many activities, this process is about the deep spring from which that stream flows. We can see how the process necessarily becomes a community affair, and to the perspective of community we must next turn our attention.

SOPHIE JENSEN'S IDENTITY FACETS

Work role facets

I am anchored and yet I'm fluid, as I **weave people and thoughts and inspiration together** with a group of recent hires, making them engage, enjoy, reflect, and, I hope, settle more into themselves.

I'm completely in the moment and, while drawing on knowledge and experience, there is also a high degree of **responding dynamically and intuitively** as I work to **expand and positively shape spheres of influence.**

Learning and **exploring deeply** for myself and in ways that surprise and intrigue me, led by something **intuitive**, which pairs the power of my mind with something essential in my heart and gut – and **weaving together the threads and sharing** that with others.

Signature skill facets

My talent is **growing people**, engaging with and caring for them *as* **people, expanding perspectives**, earning their respect and trust.

My talent is **planning and orchestrating in real-time group discussions** that put people at ease and weave together multiple perspectives into something united and whole and forward-moving.

My talent is **creating structure out of abstract thoughts** and capturing it in **compelling writing**

COMMUNITY

Human reality is relational reality. We are always in relationship, even when our senses would seem to indicate that we are "alone." Buddhists remind us that all life is interdependent, and many of the great twentieth-century psychologists wrote extensively on the way relationships make us the person that we are. Our being, from the beginning, is communal and all work is done in community. Community is an archetype of working life that demands our attention, for it is always present.

Each of us is faced with the task of understanding what work community means for us. Are we energized in a highly competitive professional environment? Do we respond better when warmth and collaboration are the established norms? Do we like the predictability and clear rules of formal hierarchical structures or do we like more informal "flat" organizations where communication across levels of seniority is encouraged? In smaller companies the force of the personalities of leaders is magnified; in larger companies established procedures, formal human resources structures, and the sheer complexity of the organization mitigate that effect. This chapter will allow you to understand more deeply and explicitly what you already know about the types of work communities where you will thrive more fully.

Successful organizations deliberately build a community that attracts the right people to get the work done and to allow the organization to grow by their efforts and their loyalty. This building of community is a paramount task of all exceptional leaders. In 2018, when Drew Faust was stepping down as the President of Harvard, she made a farewell visit to the Business School faculty. One of the attendees asked her to comment on what she felt was most important when leading an organization as large and diverse as Harvard, long known for the independence of its various schools. She responded with a parable. A visitor to a city came upon three workers, all engaged in what seemed to be the same task of cutting stone. She asked the first, "What are you doing"? His reply: "I am cutting stone." She asked the same question to the second, who replied, "I am building a wall." "What are you doing?" she asked for the third time to the remaining worker. "I am building a cathedral."

The novelist, poet, and essayist Wendell Berry writes extensively about the essential human task of realizing community.

We are all "members," he has said, and he goes on to point out that some of us know it, and some of us do not. Berry's essays and novels reveal the profound healing quality that comes with this full recognition of belonging. All three workers are building a cathedral. The difference is that the third worker *knows* that he is building a cathedral and for this reason his experience of work is vastly enriched. He taps into an energy and a sense of belonging that is less available to the first two workers. He is far less likely to become alienated and estranged from his work, even when difficulties such as a new boss with an attitude, longer hours to meet a deadline, or no raises for several years, arise. He will be far less likely to turn to addiction in the face of anger, frustration, and disappointment. Those who know they belong participate in a larger sense of life. Community is always there; our participation and awareness are always in need of cultivation.

Work community is typically spoken of in terms of *organizational culture*. This is a fluid and rather encompassing term that constitutes its own subfield within the study of organizational behavior. It has been defined in different ways by different theorists, but it generally refers to the social environments that organizations create, consciously or not, as they organize themselves to get work done. Creating an effective culture is universally seen as a primary contributor to organizational success. The character of culture varies widely across organizations and it is constituted on different levels. When I am working with my students, I often suggest that they analyze a company's culture at four levels.

The first level is that of the industry itself. Industries, even though the companies within them vary considerably, tend to share general cultural characteristics. At this high level of analysis, highly competitive "star system" Investment Banks tend to differ from extremely customer-centric Hospitality organizations and both differ from the expertise–driven and more volatile environments often found at high-technology start-ups. The second level of culture analysis is that of the company itself. Companies strive to create recognizable and sustainable cultures and use these cultures to attract valued workers and differentiate themselves in the marketplace. The third level of analysis is that of the business units. Business units have their own history, have leaders with differing personalities, do different work, and attract different types of people. Even within the same company, you should not expect the same culture in Sales as in Finance. Nor should you be surprised to find different cultures in each of the regional sales units. The final level of culture, and among the most potent, is that of your boss's personality.

Your first task in regard to work community is finding the organizational culture that is right for you at all four levels.

There may indeed be other elements of work that you allow to take priority: job title, compensation trajectory, proximity to home, or growth opportunity, to name a few. Sometimes the force of the Necessity archetype holds sway and you join a particular work community because it is the only one that seems available given all of the demands at play in your life. My experience has been that, when they are able, people place increasing value on organizational culture as they grow in work experience. This is a lesson often learned the hard way, through experiences with difficult bosses or in cultures that are uninspiring if not downright stifling. The essence of cultivating work community is coming to understand what types of organizational cultures work for you, seeking them out, contributing to their maintenance, and, if necessary, seeking new settings when a formerly desirable culture undergoes a radical change.

There have been many different attempts to understand the fundamental elements of organizational culture. One of the more durable comes from the work of Geert Hofstede, who identified six essential dimensions of organizational culture. Models such as Hofstede's are very useful in that they can guide our own introspection about where we are most comfortable on each of the dimensions. They also provide a framework for the comparative study of organizational cultures. We, however, will remain faithful to the process of this book and will not begin by trying to fit your life into preexisting categories. Our process is one that will allow you to derive your own model of organizational culture based on your lived experience.

The decade of our twenties in particular is a time of experimentation and discovery in the realm of community. It is a time of great learning about the types of people we want to be around, at work and in life generally. Initially, it is a process of trial and error. We take a job ostensibly for one reason and through experience begin to learn about the many things that come together to make the total reality of our experience at work. We begin to see that certain work settings attract certain types of people with certain types of interests, that certain organizations have shared values or styles of communication, have hierarchies that are relatively dense or relatively flat, and have more or less flexibility in the way things get done.

We learn that organizations, because of the way they are organized and because of the people who are there, are more or less able to handle the stresses that are part and parcel of their arena of operations. We learn that there are skilled and thoughtful managers and that there are bosses who are neither. I remember well the "crash course" in the importance of workplace culture that I had early in my career when I unwittingly stepped into a poorly managed and highly conflicted academic department. Whether or not we organize our thinking about our experience, we, through our lived experience, come to an implicit understanding of the issues of organizational culture generally. We also come to an understanding about what's important for *us* in terms of our working environment.

This learning continues as our experience grows. When I am counseling an executive in her forties or fifties, I am working with someone who knows a great deal more about herself and about the workplace cultures that work for her than twenty- or thirty-year-olds generally. The executive in her forties or fifties will also know more than the thirty-year-old version of herself. What she knows, however, often exists as implicit intelligence and is not fully available to her. My counseling work often involves a process that allows my client to find accurate new language for what is already available from experience. I will often ask my clients to talk about work cultures that they enjoyed and to "tell me more," prompting them to go deeper and find just the right words that describe cultures that drew them in and both challenged and supported them. I will ask them to talk, as well, about cultures that they found alienating, with the same intent to find new language.

When my clients engage in this process they come to realize that they do, in fact, know more about what nourishes them and what stifles them than they had previously recognized. They come to see that they have been carrying an unarticulated perspective on good and bad (for them) organizational cultures that needs to be taken to the next step of actually naming the culture dimensions that are most salient for them, whether expressed positively or negatively. When they take this next step, they are actually moving their implicit perspective to a higher level of knowing, to the level of explicated theory, their own *personal* theory of organizational culture.

This is a powerful step. It allows them to recognize the essential underlying patterns of what they had, until this effort, known only implicitly. With fresh language for these patterns, they can now fully own, and fully use, what they know. They can compare the organizational culture of one job to another, using consistent and repeatable frames of reference. They have created their own theory of organizational culture from their own hard-won lived experience. By following the steps in the exercise below, you can do the same.

YOUR OWN THEORY OF ORGANIZATIONAL CULTURE

As we have said, you already know a lot about the types of work cultures that are right for you. We will be "mining" this implicit knowledge and turning the ore that we find into the gold of fresh new language, in the form of an explicit theory, for what you need most from a work community. We will begin from a place of free attention. Please turn now to Appendix II to be guided into a place of free attention if you want to move through the exercise by reading the text itself. Alternatively, if you visit www.fourelementsbook.com, I will lead you through the process for using free attention and then step you through the exercise itself.

STEP 1. Writing from a Deeply Remembered Time of Positive Work Community

From the place of a concentrated returning to the middle of your body, holding an open curiosity of how things are right now, allow a memory to form of a time at work when you felt a strong sense of belonging and connection with the people and atmosphere of your workplace. Let this suggestion come into your field of attention as it is anchored in the middle of your body: Allow a memory to form of a time when you felt "at home" at work. A time when you felt that you were with like-minded people that you wanted to spend time with. A time when you looked forward to being at your workplace with the people that would be there. Do not editorialize or pick or choose. Allow a memory image to come and work from that one. How is it now in the middle of the body? Allow a felt sense to form "a direct, bodily-felt, unclear edge" of what being " at home at work" was like. No need for words or analysis. How is it, this deep body feel of being part of a positive work community? If you are relatively young and do not have significant work community experience, you may choose a work community that you have heard about or admired from a distance.

Go inside, focusing on how this memory feels in the middle of your body. Stay with it, returning your attention to the feeling in the middle of the body each time you get caught up in thoughts or other distractions. Allow a felt sense, a distinct bodily-felt unclear edge, to form about what it was like at that time. Stay with the felt sense, even if the sensation itself begins to change. It is fine if images and memories come from more than one work culture that you have experienced. Perhaps no work culture "had it all" for you, so these images from different experiences will be helpful.

From the felt sense, allow **five adjectives** to emerge, one at a time and taking your time, that describe the **people and the atmosphere** of that workplace, or those workplaces, where you felt most at home, most connected. Try to find just the right adjective to capture your felt sense. When you have done this, examine your list of adjectives. If you have two adjectives that are close to being synonyms, such as "informal" and "relaxed," pick the one that resonates most with your felt sense of your experience and drop the other. Replace the dropped adjective with another by returning to your felt sense and allowing a new word to emerge.

STEP 2. Find the Non-Negative Opposite for Each of Your Adjectives

For each adjective you have chosen, find the right word that represents its opposite quality stated positively. For example, if your adjective were "energetic," do not select a pejorative such as "listless" but rather a word that suggests a positive opposite of high energy such as "calm." Take your time. After selecting each opposite adjective, check your adjective pair against your felt sense by returning to your felt sense of your positive work culture and making sure that both adjectives, the one you chose and its opposite, both feel right. Replace any adjective that does not resonate with one that better represents the felt sense of what you mean. If you realize at this stage that two of your adjective pairs are very close in their meaning, drop one pair and repeat Step One to find a new positive adjective and its non-negative opposite. At the end of this step you will have five word pairs, each composed of a word that expresses a quality of work culture that you find compelling and a word that expresses its opposite in a non-pejorative way.

STEP 3. Naming Your Essential Dimensions of Work Culture

This step is the crucial step of naming, using fresh new language, each of the five dimensions represented by your adjective opposite pairs. The adjectives in each of your word pairs anchor the extremes of a dimension of work culture that is important for you. Your dimensions do not yet have names.

Your task is to name each. To take a very abstract example, if one adjective was "hot" and the other "cold," the best dimension name would be "temperature." If your pair were "high" and "low," a good dimension name would be "altitude." Naming each dimension will allow you to have precise language for an aspect of work culture that is essential for you. Finding just the right dimension name is important; it must be your language. To take my own personal example from the sidebar, I had arrived at the word pair of "warm" and "reserved." After returning to my felt sense of what I was trying to mean, I eventually arrived at the dimension name of *Intimacy*. The extent to which the people at a workplace are open to relationship is indeed essential for me. You can see the names I arrived at for my other dimensions in the sidebar itself.

Try an initial word for each dimension. Then return to your felt sense of being in a good work community and see if that dimension name resonates. If it seems off, not quite right, return to the felt sense and see what other word, or phrase, emerges that better captures the name of that dimension. Do this as many times as you need until the dimension name, no matter how unusual, seems right. At the end of this step you will have named your five most important work community dimensions, the extremes of which are anchored by your adjective pair for each dimension.

STEP 4. Check for a Missing Dimension(s)

With your list of dimensions in front of you, return to your felt sense of your positive work community experience. From this place, as you look at your list, allow the question to form: "Is there something missing from my list?" A dimension might be missing for several reasons. It may have been poorly represented even at your most positive work community experience. It may not have made your "top five" adjective list even though now, upon reflection, you realize that it is essential. If you sense a missing dimension, repeat the adjective pair process, first selecting the adjective that describes the important missing quality and then finding a non-negative opposite. Complete the process by naming the dimension as in Step 3 and then add it to your final list of essential work community dimensions.

STEP 5. Create a Positive Work Community Narrative

With your list of essential work community dimensions in front of you, begin to write, freely providing more detail and examples of what each one means to you. You might want to revisit different work communities that you have experienced and "score" each on your dimensions. You might want to think and write about how you can assess a potential work community for each dimension. By using your dimensions as a compositional structure, create a vivid portrait about what a positive work community means to you at this moment in your life.

SOPHIE JENSEN

Community Deep Dive

STEP 1. Writing from a Deeply Remembered Time of Positive Work Community
From the felt sense, allow **five adjectives** to emerge, one at a time and taking your time, that describe the **people and the atmosphere** of that workplace.

Personal
Supportive
Camaraderie
Engaged
Reflective

STEP 2. Find the Non-Negative Opposite for Each of Your Adjectives
Personal <> detached
Encouraging <> judgmental
Camaraderie <> serious
Engaged <> impartial
Reflective <>transactional

STEP 3. Naming Your Essential Dimensions of Work Culture
Intimacy: personal <> formal
Interpersonal attitude: encouraging <> judgmental
Interpersonal energy: camaraderie <> exclusively task focused
Personal meaning: engaged <> impartial
Mental model: reflective <> transactional

STEP 4. Check for a Missing Dimension(s)
Intellectual scope: stimulating <> known
Mission: build <> priority for profit

STEP 5. Create a Positive Work Community
Narrative
Overall, I'm most engaged when I'm in a community of "real people" who want the best for, and see the best in, one another. They laugh, learn, care, and create; all in the service of "makinsg a difference."

Intimacy
I want to work in a community of people, not projections. Do colleagues allow themselves to be seen as real, three-dimensional people – and are they interested in seeing me that way? Are they interesting, and interested?

Interpersonal attitude
I most enjoy communities with a supportive instinct to enable and empower, not solely "evaluate." Do they listen and perceive with generosity or judgement? Do they genuinely see the best in others?

Interpersonal energy
I want there to be room for laughter and friendship, rather than being surrounded by either masks or frowns. Even in my toughest work moments, having a sense of camaraderie with my colleagues made me laugh instead of cry. Do they have a sense of humor and perspective? Are we in this together?

Personal meaning
I want people to have some skin in the game; to care; to feel that the work we are doing matters. I don't want to work with mercenaries. Do people believe in what we're doing? Do they have a larger narrative for what this means to them? Are they intentional about even being here and doing this?

Mental model
I want to work with people who are deeply engaged in the journey, not just the destination. What are we learning? What does it mean? I don't want to only be "heads down" and executing. I want to be in an environment with thinking, alongside the action.

Intellectual scope
I enjoy communities of creation, where we are collectively exploring the unknown or finding new ways of looking at the "known." Do we structure otherwise ambiguous and unarticulated fields? Do we and others think and see differently as a result of our work?

Mission
I want to be part of something bigger than my company or projects. What is the point of what we're doing? To me, this means working collectively to "build" or contribute something to society or the world, rather than just to gain a bigger slice of an existing pie.

This five-step exercise does not produce a universal model of the essential and irreducible elements of organizational culture such as those derived by Hofstede and other organizational psychologists. When you have finished this process you will have identified the dimensions of work community and organizational culture that are essential *for you*. It is an explication or model that makes objective and knowable what you have learned implicitly from your unique working-life experience. As you continue to work, your experience will increase and your world, at work and outside of work, will become more intricate.

If you continue to do the type of inquiry that is being introduced in this book, your understanding, as well, has the potential to become more intricate and nuanced. It is likely that the dimensions that have emerged from this exercise will remain important for you, but your understanding of them will grow and you may discover others. By continuing this type of reflection, you will also become more adept at assessing where a potential workplace falls on each of your essential work community dimensions. If you keep this spirit of inquiry alive, you will become better and better at finding an organizational culture that is right for you.

SEARCHING FOR YOUR WORK CULTURE MATCH

Getting a handle on the actual work culture of a potential employer is difficult. If you are a serious candidate, or if the competition for talent is high because of a good economy, any organization is likely to place an emphasis on the virtues of its culture. Add to this the complexity of the need to evaluate culture at all four of its levels: industry, company, business unit, and the personality of your boss. Although there are traits that many would agree are highly desirable for most organizations, there is no universal good culture. A culture that may be good for a friend or colleague is not necessarily good for you; that is why doing the work outlined in this chapter is an essential first step before beginning a job search. When you are asking questions of people familiar with the organization that you are trying to evaluate, generic questions will not only not help, they will most likely elicit familiar, abstract, "buzzword" answers. You must ask *your* questions that come out of your particular essential dimensions of work-life culture.

In order to evaluate a work culture, you need to get close to it. This can be difficult given the timeline of a typical job search. You may have only a handful of interviews before you are asked for a decision on an offer. You probably will not have the opportunity to spend much time in the actual space where you will be working before you must make a decision. It is important to speak to as many people as possible and spend as much time as possible onsite before you must make a decision. What you are seeking is a deeper "body feel" for what it is actually like to show up every day and work at that particular place with the particular people who will constitute your new work community. If you receive an offer, you can communicate your excitement about the opportunity, but at the same time, ask to speak with a few more people about the job and express a strong preference for doing this in person at the workplace. As a guide, the sidebar gives a brief summary of what I would look for as evidence of each of my own positive work community dimensions.

In the accompanying side box, I provide an example of how I would evaluate a potential organizational culture on the six culture dimensions that emerged when I participated in this exercise: *Intimacy, Creativity, Quality Priority, Intensity, Intellectual Bias,* and *Values Priority.*

Author's Example of Evaluating an Organization for Personal Positive Work Environment Dimensions

Intimacy. What I am looking for in this dimension goes beyond evidence that people seem to enjoy working at a particular organization. That is, of course, very important but it is not sufficient evidence that an organization offers intimacy. What I am looking for is evidence that the culture has selected people who value the *relational* aspects of their day-to-day work. Are office doors open or closed? How do people greet each other in the hallways? On my interview visits do I observe people engaging in conversation? Do I overhear conversations about personal lives? Do people seem to be genuinely listening in these conversations? In interviews, are my interviewers good listeners, or do they seem to work their way through a formal interview protocol? Do they seem genuinely interested in me and my personal situation? Are birthdays celebrated in the office? Is this the sort of place where someone would be encouraged to bring their partner, child, or favorite pet in for an introduction to colleagues? Most importantly, is there a palpable sense of warmth that characterizes the interactions that I have and observe?

Creativity. An assessment for creativity hinges on determining whether or not workers are primarily rewarded for the execution of tried and true processes and procedures or are given significant latitude to meet goals using the means that they can best devise to do so. Also vital is the extent to which an organization must innovate in order to survive and thrive. Is the market in their area highly competitive? Is it highly dynamic and undergoing disruptions that call for novel responses? Is the product cycle short and the demand for new products or service offerings high? These latter questions are indeed researchable. Good questions to ask are how the business is different from what it was two years ago and what the challenges are that will shape the business for the next two years.

Every organization must "get out the laundry" and execute well on basic work processes that have a history of being effective. They will vary greatly, however, on the extent to which they must be nimble because of changing markets and customer demands. They will also vary on the philosophy of senior management in regard to individual initiative. Typically, the prerogative of personal initiative grows with seniority and rank. This means that a good place to focus observation is on the more junior levels of the organization. Do younger employees seem to be more empowered compared to what you would expect?

Quality Priority. I want to work for an organization that is known for doing something very well. Unless there are interfering currents from other aspects of the organization (personalities of senior leaders, respect for worker initiative and wellbeing, etc.) this will inevitably translate into workers who are proud of their organization. Do I sense this pride at all levels of the organization? To a certain extent, quality is a researchable dimension. What is the reputation of the organization? Is it a standout in its field? Does my experience with the organization's product or service *consistently* impress me? Are their communications with me professional and timely? Do they handle the details of the interview process with thoughtfulness? As I walk the halls and visit offices during the interview process is there care given to the orderliness and quality of the environment? Later, I will look for evidence of data-driven decisions and the continual use of metrics to evaluate performance and end-user experience.

Intensity. I want to work for an organization that works hard and is serious about its business. I want it to be an organization that pivots quickly to meet new challenges and increases its efforts in the face of these challenges. This quality is difficult to evaluate without significant time spent at the organization, but there are some signs that can be indicators. During the interview process, is there a definite "buzz" at the workplace? Do people seem focused and serious? What is my "body feel" for the general energy level? Do people work late and on weekends? (This latter point raises the question of work-life balance. You need to know where you stand on that important dimension, being clear on how much demand for employee time is excessive in your view and, at the other extreme, how much signals a lack of serious commitment to the organization's mission).

Intellectual Bias. This dimension may have as much to do with my particular role as it does with the organization as a whole. That being said, I want to work for an organization whose mandate is to analyze, innovate, explore, discover, learn, and apply what is learned to better service or a better product. As in my evaluation of *Quality Priority*, I will look for evidence of data-driven decisions and the continual use of metrics to evaluate performance and end-user experience. I will look for evidence of quick implementation of new knowledge. I will need a clear signal from my hiring manager that I am being selected to work on problems that present significant intellectual challenge.

Values Priority. This is a dimension where research can indeed help. What is the word on the street about how this organization does business? Does a thorough Google search reveal any legal or ethical issues of note? What about a search on the backgrounds of senior leaders and the leaders of my work group? Is the brand of the organization well respected? This latter point is important in that protecting a hard-earned brand image is a powerful incentive for ethical vigilance.

NECESSITY

Marco Rossi grew up in the Bensonhurst section of Brooklyn, NY, where his father was able to grow his bakery into a modestly successful business by the time Marco was five years old. His mother was an elementary school teacher. Early on, Marco was seen by the wider family circle as "the smart one" amongst his cousins. He was focused and earnest, a standout in the classroom from the beginning. He excelled in math in particular. His parents encouraged him every step of the way and when he tested into the elite Stuyvesant High School, he assumed the role within the family of the one who was destined for bigger things.

From Stuyvesant, Marco went to Princeton, where he was an Economics major. He chose the consulting path after college and landed a highly competitive position with McKinsey& Company. I first met him when he was a student at Harvard Business School, and he stayed in touch after graduating, having returned to McKinsey for two years before transitioning to a strategic planning role at a rapidly growing online retailer with headquarters in New York. This led to a significant management position with that company and several promotions in the ensuing years. It had been fourteen years since his Harvard graduation when I received an email from him asking if we could have a counseling session.

Two months prior to our conversation, an executive search firm had called him to discuss what sounded like a very exciting opportunity. A former boss had recommended him highly for a position leading a major new initiative for a company that was growing rapidly. The job sounded like everything that Marco had been longing for: a high-stakes senior leadership role that would be central to the success of the larger company. He would be the division president for a business that was going to be central to the company's new strategy. There were indeed problems with the division as several key players had left after the brief and tumultuous tenure of the most recent president. Marco would have his hands full in rebuilding the team while at the same time pushing to meet the aggressive goals set out by senior management. For the first year, maybe longer, he would be spending long hours at the office. He sent me the email when that same headhunter called to tell him that the job was his if he wanted it. When I picked up the phone for that session, I could tell right away that he was in the midst of a struggle.

Why, given his obvious excitement as he described the offer, was he calling me? He continued with his story. His oldest child, Tony, was now fourteen and would be entering high school in the fall. School had not come as easily for him as for Marco, and the onset of adolescence had been tough for him. His grades had dropped and Mark did not approve of his choice of friends. He felt that both he and his wife had a solid relationship with Tony, but both were worried. In recent weeks it had become clear to Marco that, contrary to his notion that older children were less demanding of parental time, Tony needed more of his presence now, not less.

When the job offer came through, the wrestling match began. Marco began to plan how he could organize his new workday to be home at least some weekday evenings during the predicted difficult first year. He would do his best to protect some weekend time to get to as many of Tony's sporting events as possible. He and his wife spoke at length about coordinating their schedules. Marco would go to bed sure that it would work out, but wake up with doubts. How could it be that the two things that were most charged with meaning for him, his children and a leadership role, could be set in opposition this way? Surely there was a way.

Marco had been speaking on the phone with me for about half an hour, making the case for both taking the job and not, when I was struck by a strong impression: Marco had already made his decision, in fact he had made it before he called me, but *he was not yet aware that he had done so.* At his next pause, I shared this. "Marco, it really seems that you have already made your decision." Even over the phone, I could sense the tears in his long silence. "Yes, you're right." Another silence. "I must be there for Tony."

At this, Marco dropped all of the activity of his analytical mind. All of the "pros" and "cons" fell away. Planning, speculation, and reasoning no longer mattered. What Marco needed to do now was grieve, and this grieving began immediately. He would be giving up something big, with no guarantees it would return. For now, he would not be waking up in the morning with the career challenge of a lifetime in front of him. Of course, both Marco and I understood that with his background and experience, more opportunities would come, but to use that right now as a rationalization would prevent him from doing what he needed to do. He needed to say goodbye to something that he wanted very much and to feel the loss deeply so that he could fully let it go.

OBLIGATION AND NECESSITY

What Marco had realized was that his obligation to Tony was both a strong desire and a necessity. For most of the time our obligations operate "in the background," without any need to be specifically called out and identified. They are there and they are real, so much so that in our day-to-day lives we have little need to examine or explore them at depth because they are taken for granted. This can all change on very short notice. Marco, of course, never did not know that he had a profound obligation to his children; the crisis set off by his job offer required that he turn toward what he knew implicitly and examine it deeply. He was both surprised and not surprised by its depth and power.

In my work as a psychotherapist and counselor I have many times encountered the experience when an obligation that has previously been invisible becomes suddenly crystallized, fully recognized, and undeniable. In eighth grade science class I was fascinated by the demonstration of the phenomenon of a super-saturated solution. The solution exists as a liquid in the test tube, but the salt dissolved in the liquid is so concentrated that a force or a blow, such as a tapping on the side of the test tube, turns the solution immediately and completely solid. This is the way it often is with life's obligations. A life force or a blow, or a decision that needs to be made, makes clear to us where our deepest commitments truly lie.

When an obligation is revealed as being non-negotiable, we recognize it as a necessity. We tend to use this word, *necessity*, casually to refer to our immediate needs for survival. In the latter part of the twentieth century, however, our collective understanding of human necessity shifted as sociologists and psychologists drew a more nuanced portrait of what was necessary to live a fully realized human life. Perhaps the most enduring model from this era is that of Abraham Maslow, who began with our basic physiological needs and the need for safety and expanded them to include the needs of the social and spiritual beings that we are. He convincingly argued that human needs extended to include the needs for love and belonging, esteem, and self-actualization (he later added the need for transcendence).

These latter categories, although not attainable without securing our most basic survival needs, are not just embellishments, but are fundamental requirements for being fully human. Maslow's need-dimensions of love and belonging, esteem, and self-actualization can only be met within a social context. Beyond our obligations to keep ourselves biologically alive and safe lies the obligation not only for us to secure the survival and safety of those we love, but to secure a sense of belonging, esteem, and self-actualization with them and for them as well.

Maslow's categories are not the rigid pyramid that many imagine them to be. They are correlated with one another and there are times when higher-order needs can supersede and interact with lower ones. Because we are social interdependent beings, the locus of the need is spread out amongst ourselves and those around us. This combination of inter-correlation and ambiguous locus makes an obligation a complex interaction rather than a static transaction. My need to meet the health needs of my child is intimately related to my self-actualization need as an effective parent. In the case of Marco and Tony, Tony's safety, esteem, and belonging needs were part and parcel of Marco's belonging and self-actualization needs. It is not possible to isolate individual actors when it comes to obligation and need events. The very words "obligation" and "need" convey ideas that are at the same time different and inseparable, like that super-saturated solution that is a liquid until it is not.

In this sense, a necessity is an obligation that has been "crystalized" in our awareness as something that we must do. When we recognize an obligation as non-negotiable we come to see it as what our life demands of us at this moment, driven as it may be one or more of Maslow's need-dimensions. In my professional experience, obligation is most often voiced in the language of money, health, belonging, and spirit. These words clearly mirror Maslow's categories, but, in keeping with the approach of this book, I would stick close to experience itself rather than impose a theory that would prematurely encapsulate our inquiry into the true nature of necessity. When considering the discussion of the dimensions of obligation that follows, please remember that any particular obligation event is likely to involve more than one dimension spread amongst the actors in the event.

DIMENSIONS OF NECESSITY

Health

Health, of ourselves and loved ones, is a primary obligation. I have heard it expressed in different ways and in different contexts. One client had a special needs child who, after a long search, had found just the right treatment resources in the local community. When an attractive work opportunity arrived elsewhere, he realized that it must be refused; the obligation to his child prevailed. Another client had made the decision to leave the major metropolitan area where she had been living. She had been receiving treatment for her breast cancer at a renowned hospital in her area and knew how to recognize the features of excellent care. She limited her job search to cities that had highly regarded cancer treatment centers. Many times I have worked with students and clients who eventually came to the conclusion that their current work setting, as interesting and otherwise rewarding as it might be, was just too stressful and a change was no longer just desirable, but was now a necessity.

Health also includes an obligation to a rhythm and routine of life that sustains us and those around us and is itself sustainable. Through the years, I have worked with many clients who have tested the limits of this obligation and learned the consequences the hard way. Many work environments make extraordinary demands during peak work periods or when a crisis emerges, but some take their workers to their limits on a "business-as-usual" basis. There is a great deal of individual variation in terms of stress and resilience. I know some hospital workers who work long shifts, and sometimes shifts back-to-back, in exchange for longer periods away from work with their families. For others, this arrangement would be intolerable. Many professionals I have worked with are willing to travel extensively, but only if that travel can be planned in advance so that family needs can be aligned with their schedules. For others, extensive travel poses a real threat to their family homeostasis. We need to learn what works for us and those closest to us, and what does not.

Belonging

Maslow included the need to belong and to love and be loved among his essential human needs. We each have our own pattern and priority of belonging. Some obligations for belonging, such as with parents, life partners, and children, are archetypal, though even these too are subject to considerable variation. What is a tolerable time away from my spouse or child for me may not be so for you. Some are estranged from family members, and other social bonds emerge to take the place of what has been lost. The character and demands of belonging change as life circumstances change. The needs of our children are quite different at ages four, eighteen, and thirty. The illness of a family member may, in a moment, change what is demanded of us to fulfill our obligation to take care of those closest to us in our net of belonging. Much has been written recently about the "sandwich generation" that simultaneously faces the demands of child- or grandchild-raising and the needs of elderly parents. These are all examples of shifting patterns of our obligation to belong.

The nature of the need to belong, and its attending obligation, can express itself uniquely in unanticipated ways. Once a senior colleague of mine told me a story about a life event that brought clarity, deeper commitment, and a strong definition of obligation to his spouse. Much earlier in his career, Sam was a young and successful executive. Offers for more senior roles in other companies began to come his way. One very attractive offer would require relocation. He was at a point where this could be the beginning of a chain reaction of advancement that offered exposure to new challenges in different cities. His wife, Carol, was also at an inflection point in her career. Her psychotherapy practice had grown substantially as her reputation spread in their area. After years of building her professional identity, she was now very much in demand. The structure of her career, however, was quite different from that of Sam's. A psychotherapy practice is not transportable.

After long discussions it became clear that the price of the rewards of intimacy and belonging had just been raised. Both Sam and Carol were deeply committed to their work. They were even more committed to each other. Fortunately, they were living in a major metropolitan area that was very attractive to both. It was not a matter of compromise; the path forward seemed to show itself. Sam had opportunities for advancement that did not require relocation. The decision was made: Sam would forge his career in the Chicago area exclusively given the particular demands of Carol's profession. The obligation of a marriage commitment that allowed for their mutual professional flourishing was seen as a non-negotiable obligation; it was revealed to be a necessity.

Financial Security

When my students and clients talk about obligations they often use the word "money" as a substitution for a vague sense of necessities that have not been fully examined and articulated. Money, of course, could represent many needs (healthcare, safety, esteem, etc.) expressed in terms of the legal tender that is believed necessary to secure them. The operative word in the preceding sentence is "believed." When it comes to money, surprisingly few people have done the hard work of discovering how much money they actually *need*. In our highly (and increasingly so) competitive global capitalist society the words "money" and "needs" have unconsciously become substitutes for one another. But what is this money for? What is the real obligation? How much money will you need to live the life that really matters?

For sure, the money that you will need will include many components – basic food and clothing needs, rent or a home payment in a neighborhood where your child can attend good schools, healthcare, sufficient funds for recreation and travel to be with extended family members, etc. The surprising thing is that these are largely researchable issues and so few actually do the research. In the absence of that research, the default answer to the "How much money do I need?" question is, "I don't really know and life is uncertain, so I better make as much money as possible." Once that belief, conscious or unconscious, is in place, money becomes the driver of work and life decisions. Issues of Identity, Community, and Horizon take a back seat. When we are feeling that more money is indeed a necessity, we should check to make sure that pure fear is not the author of this conclusion. We need money and, unless we want to be the slaves of this fear, we have some math work to do.

Spirit

Obligations of spirit are often less obvious and harder to pin down than their more utilitarian siblings, but they are no less compelling. They come in different guises and, like the other obligation dimensions, are often not fully grasped until challenged. Maslow placed "self-actualization" at the top of his hierarchy of human needs (and, as I said before, he later added a need for "transcendence"), but that is not the term I would use for what I have observed in my students and other clients over the years. It has a ring that is too abstract and clinical. What I see is more akin to a deep passion or yearning. Like the need of one student to do *anything* necessary to position herself to eventually found a start-up in the education sector. Or the person who realizes that his job search must be limited to cities that will allow his passion for mountain climbing to be fulfilled. Or the graduate student who planned her medical career to lead as soon as possible back to the vibrant church community that had nourished her and her family when she was growing up. Or the person who *must* live in the city of her dreams.

An obligation of spirit is an obligation to something that seems more powerful, enlivening, and important than what can be understood with the analytical mind. Why does someone feel compelled to climb mountains? To worship at a particular church, synagogue, or mosque? To adopt a child with severe special needs even when one has healthy children of one's own? To study a particular author? To put other things aside so that she can live in a particular place? It is something that simultaneously feels essential and inexplicable. Because of this at times ineffable nature of spirit, it is often difficult for our significant others to understand the depth of its hold on us. It is important that we try to explain because in doing so we find new language for our own experience and it brings us closer to understanding the nature of this powerful force in our lives. Equally, it is our task to be patient and listen deeply when others are trying to explain to us their own obligations of spirit, and to do our best to honor them even if the experience we are hearing them describe is not our own experience.

We can see obligations of spirit writ large in some exemplary leaders. Mother Theresa had no choice, her obligation to serve the poorest of the poor was all consuming. No other priority could challenge Nelson Mandela's total dedication to bringing about the end to apartheid. The obligations of the spirit I have heard articulated in my work have not been as grand and consequential as these, but they have held no less meaning for those who had come to recognize their necessity. The stuff of obligations of the spirit truly belongs in the realm covered in our next chapter, *Horizon*. It would be remiss, however, not to introduce them here, for there are times in life when they bring their own urgency of necessity.

THE GRAVITATIONAL FIELD OF NECESSITY

Necessity acts in our lives with a force similar to that of gravity. It holds us firmly to the earth and our real world, preventing our myriad desires and fantasies from launching us into ethereal places. It keeps us grounded and reminds us, often abruptly, of what is most important. As you sit reading this book, you are most likely unaware of gravity's extraordinary effect on your existence, but it is there, and you ignore it at your peril. Necessity is no different. As the gravitational fields of celestial bodies shape time and space, so necessity shapes the curve of our work and life decision-making. It does this both in undramatic, often unconscious, day-to-day ways and in very dramatic ways when a crisis flares. When things are going badly at a job that has ceased inspiring us, and we wake up on a cold winter morning and automatically get dressed and start our routine to head to the office, we do not consciously think "I am doing all this because of the necessity of paying the rent and our children's tuition." Necessity is functioning on autopilot. Our decision to stay in a suboptimal job, or the only job that is available, has been shaped by the gravity of necessity. Our decision to live in a town, rather than our preferred city setting, because of its school system, is another example of a decision shaped by necessity.

There are times when new choices emerge because what was formerly necessary no longer is. We do not always catch onto this right away. The requirements of those who were in need of our attention, energy, and support change, but we continue living and making decisions in a force field of obligation that has continued for us automatically. The opposite can also be true. In the case of Marco, the force field of Tony's needs had subtly and gradually grown stronger before Marco and his wife became fully aware of its implications. As life changes, our commitments and obligations also change. For this reason, it's important that we have an accurate and deep feel for the center of gravity of our current necessity. What follows is a process for doing so that unfolds in two parts. The first part of the process is intended to allow you to clearly visualize the important people in your field of obligation. The second part is a process for generating fresh new language for what truly are your most pressing nonnegotiable commitments at this moment in time. We will begin from a place of free attention. Please turn now to Appendix II to be guided into a place of free attention if you want to move through the exercise by reading the text itself. Alternatively, if you visit www.fourelementsbook.com, I will lead you through the process for using free attention and then step you through the exercise itself.

YOUR REALMS OF BELONGING

As a first step in finding new language for how you understand your obligations, imagine a diagram of three concentric circles. The first circle is you. You have obligations to yourself from all four of the categories (money, belonging, health, spirit). The next circle represents your immediate circle of care. Within that circle are the people that comprise your closest and most intimate social world; you have obligations in all four of the obligation categories to these people as well. Frequent denizens of this circle often include a partner or significant other, children, parents, and others with whom you have a particularly strong bond. The outermost circle is a circle of your extended network of caring. It is quite possible for people in your life to move from one circle to another. A good friend or relative might inhabit the outer circle until life events move them into an inner circle of your concern.

Your task, right now, is to populate these circles. Do not use your analytical mind for this task, but rather pay attention to what comes to you as you observe what arrives as the answer to this question. You may be surprised. The process must start from a place of free attention, so please turn now to Appendix II to begin.

From this place of free attention, allow the images and names of those people who belong in your immediate circle of care to arise. Take your time, do not force the process. The first images and names will be obvious and immediate. Wait to see if other images and names arise. Do not edit with the analytical mind. If you are surprised when an unexpected image or name arrives, include that person for now. Stay with the process until you have a felt sense that the process of populating your immediate circle of care is complete.

NEW LANGUAGE FOR YOUR NECESSARY COMMITMENTS

STEP ONE

From this continuing place of free attention, allow the answer to this question to emerge: "Who in my immediate circle of obligation has needs that, right now, are most pressing?" Make sure that this answer comes spontaneously from the observing intelligence of your free attention, rather than from your analytical mind. You are looking for a felt sense of what aspect of obligation is bearing on you right now. In the middle of your body, what obligation, right now, has the biggest hold on you? Take your time.

STEP TWO

Holding the image of the person who emerged from Step One in your free attention, allow a deep felt sense to form of how this person's life is right now. Stay with the image, do not force the process. Return your attention to the center of your body and allow a deep sense of this person and his or her current circumstances to abide. With your free attention, not with your analytical mind, allow this question to emerge: "What is this person's current life asking of me, requiring of me, right now?" You can use the four categories of obligation to scan your field of experience. Is it a money issue? Is it a belonging (need for a stronger presence from you) issue? Is it a health issue? Is it an issue of spirit? Stay with the felt sense of your inquiry.

STEP THREE

From the maturing essence of your felt sense, write a fresh new sentence that is your best attempt to capture your obligation to this person right now. For those who are most intimate in your immediate circle of caring, such as a partner or child, you will probably need to write four sentences, one for each of the four dimensions of obligation. Take your time in composing each sentence. When each sentence is complete, underline one or two key words. If your sentence feels authentic, fresh, and complete, move on to Step Four. If not, for each of the underlined words, write a fresh new sentence that says what you really mean by that word. This final sentence or sentences will capture the reality of your true obligation(s), rather than your previous unexamined assumptions in regard to what this person needs from you right now.

Let the image of the person that you have been working with dissolve and return to a pure state of free attention. Check and see if the image of another person from your immediate circle of caring presents itself to you. Who else, right now, needs you? Be careful to use the intelligence of your free attention rather than that of your analytical mind. Repeat Steps Two and Three for this person. If no image of another person arises with urgency, move on to Step Four.

STEP FOUR

Explicitly, add yourself. From a place of free attention, ask each of the questions below in turn. Take your time with each, allowing a felt sense of the answer to form. From that felt sense, write a fresh new sentence that brings language to that felt sense of the answer.

- What does my desire to be healthy require from me at this time?
- What does my need for intimacy and belonging require from me at this time?
- What does my need for financial security require from me at this time?
- Am I aware of spiritual obligation(s) at this time? How would I put this obligation into words?

STEP FIVE: Creating Your Necessity Narrative

Now is the time to write freely from the felt sense of the particular way that the gravitational field of necessity holds you right now. Allow your sentences to expand and see what comes as you begin to write outward from them. Allow the writing itself to lead you into new language about the details of your most pressing obligations. Do not try to be comprehensive; this writing is about what is up front and most vital. It is not a survey of the obligations that you may recognize throughout the extended network or your belonging. Return to the felt sense whenever your writing threatens to become abstract or formulaic. What is pressing you, right now? Do you feel a tension between the obligations toward yourself and an obligation to someone in your immediate circle of care? If that is the case, hold that tension between obligation to yourself and obligation to others until a clear felt since of the tension forms. Stay with that felt sense until you can write one or more clear sentences that capture this tension. Do not force a premature resolution of this tension; it is enough to find fresh new language for the tension itself.

WORKING WITH NECESSITY

Our sense of obligation needs to let the other three essential views (Identity, Community, Horizon) breathe. Many times I have listened to a client describing possible roles that will enhance and realize identity or job settings that offer an attractive community, only to stop dead in his or her tracks: "But I really can't do that, at least not now, because . . ." The "because" is then followed by an obligation that is perceived to be a necessity that is in direct conflict with the exciting vision or opportunity. Sometimes it is, indeed, a necessity. Often, it is an obligation that has not been thoroughly vetted and placed in context. In either case, there is a way to proceed that will allow the other views to be fully appreciated, even amidst the press of true necessity.

The trick is to extend your inquiry into each of the views and allow each of them to show fully what they need to show you at this moment in time, *even if you already know that a particular necessity will have the final say*. The heart needs to show you its desire. You need to ask the deep questions about your identity (your interests and signature skills) and the community where you will thrive. You need to let the pull of the horizon of what truly matters speak fully (more on this in the next chapter). Even if you must make concessions in identity and community realization, you need to take the next steps in recognizing them more fully. That way they become projects that can continue to unfold, even if this unfolding is slowed or diverted by the demands of necessity. That way, you know that what you are doing is a sacrifice, and that sacrifice now has meaning. Meaning in fulfilling the necessity against the background of something postponed, and the meaning of knowing where you need to go when necessity abates. Work on the matters of the heart and the matters of necessity *in parallel*, and work on them fully.

If the gravitational field of necessity holds us to the earth and reminds us of what is most essential, there is another celestial-like force that exerts itself not as a press or push (as necessity often seems) but rather as a *pull*. It is a pull toward a larger and fuller life. There is something in us that wants to move toward the horizon of what we have experienced and beyond to what we might become. From time to time we look up and catch a glimpse of others who seem to have already made the journey. How do we understand what life would be in its fullest? Always present and activated at every major work and life juncture, we must now turn our attention to understanding the archetypal pull of *Horizon*.

SOPHIE JENSEN

Necessity Deep Dive

Immediate circle of care
- Mom
- Dad
- Sara
- Javier
- Emily
- Sam

1. Who in my immediate circle of obligation has needs that, right now, are most pressing?
- Dad
- Sara
- Javier

2. Dad: What is this person's current life asking of me, requiring of me, right now?
- Analysis/research/connections
- Money?
- Support/encouragement/connection

3A. My obligation to Dad right now
- Health: I need to help Dad <u>navigate</u> Medicare and his healthcare network to get the <u>best, most cost-effective</u> treatment for his ongoing health issues
- Belonging: I need to help Dad <u>not feel afraid or depressed</u> about his health challenges; I need to be <u>supportive and encouraging</u> of his physical outlook

- Financial security: I need to help Mom and Dad by potentially <u>contributing</u> to the costs of his treatment if his out-of-pocket expenses become onerous
- Spirit: I need to help Dad see this <u>isn't the end of his enjoyment</u> of trail running and that he can still enjoy and be enlivened by physical adventure

2B. Sara: What is this person's current life asking of me, requiring of me, right now?
- Encouragement
- Support
- Connection/belonging/love
- Respect/value

3B. Sara: My obligation to Sara right now
- Health: n/a
- Belonging: I need to offer Sara a sense of <u>love and belonging</u> as my cousin as well as <u>belief and encouragement</u> as she finishes her architecture course and tries to cultivate work in that space, potentially also moving abroad
- Financial security: I need to guide Sara to have a <u>full experience</u> during her time in school in London without worrying too much about money
- Spirit: I need to help Sara <u>believe in herself</u> and her own potential and value

2C. Javier: What is this person's current life asking of me, requiring of me, right now?
- Flexibility
- Patience
- Stability

- Support/encouragement
- Acceptance
- Love/warmth

3C. Javier: My obligation to Javier right now

- Health: I need to help Javier strike a <u>sustainable balance</u> between work, next-steps thinking, family, exercise, church, and travel/adventure
- Belonging: I need to be a <u>stable and warm</u> presence for Javier, especially as his work transition thinking evolves; I need to be both <u>patient and flexible</u> as he explores his own next steps and decision-making
- Financial security: I may need to help Javier <u>bridge some transition time</u> between his current job and whenever he fully moves into the family enterprises; we also need to (gradually) work toward a <u>financially sustainable joint life</u>
- Spirit: I need to support Javier's <u>church engagements</u> and his desire for <u>travel/adventure</u>

4A. What does my desire to be healthy require from me at this time?

I need enough time and energy to support my sleep, exercise, and nutrition needs, as well as my meditation and general appetite for and engagement with life; I need to keep work stress at bay and operate in a whole/integrated way where I feel connected to and valued by myself and others as a "real" person, not a robot

4B. What does my need for intimacy and belonging require from me at this time?

I need to invest sufficient time and energy into my intimate friendships and family, and cultivating stability and connection with Javier; I need to maintain a sustainable balance in life and keep building my confidence, self-esteem, and "presence" in my authentic self (i.e., not putting myself in positions where I feel cut-off from myself, under constant evaluation/judgement and "not enough")

4C. What does my need for financial security require from me at this time?
I need to be comfortably covering the basics (living expenses, health) in the immediate, as well as having confidence in the longer term (ability to buy own home) and the financial freedom to "pause" and reflect/adjust along the way; I potentially need to be in a position to help my family with healthcare costs, though I'm not sure of my real responsibility or ability here – for this and more broadly, I need greater explicit knowledge about my financial needs

4D. Am I aware of a spiritual obligation(s) at this time? How would I put this obligation into words?
I need to continue engaging and growing through my spiritual practices and exploration; I need to create the time, space, and appetite for the things that deeply energize me, especially the outdoor world and running; I also find myself thinking of children at this time and the joint journey and meaning that represents

5. My Necessity Narrative
Throughout school, I followed an organic, inquisitive, "direct experience" (vs. "outside-in" thinking) path but from the time I decided to study computer science at

college, I became much more deliberate and planned. Since then, and especially since coming across artificial intelligence toward the end of my studies, I have been driven (mostly unconsciously, I think) by financial safety, as well as "identity"/status safety. However, another transition has been underway since my time in graduate school, accelerating in the past ~6 months. I feel an imperative for myself to live a more whole, integrated, "well," joyous life. I feel an immense tension between this and my desire for financial safety – partly for myself but mostly for my family.

At the time I decided to study computer science (about 10 years ago), I carved an identity for myself that felt financially secure and technologically sophisticated. I feel nervous about stepping out of the lucrative world of enterprise software and perhaps even corporate work completely – both because of what it might signal of my own financial future, and also because it lessens my ability to be at the cutting edge of the world's technological advances.

I also feel a huge tension in my own desires/needs and the obligations to my relationship with Javier. He deeply wants to chart a course back to Mexico and I've come to accept that's something I at least need to try. But that seems to curtail much of what compels me – my family and friends here, trail running in the Pacific Northwest, my current work, and what I'm starting to explore with Immigration Law and the UN.

Even within my own needs/desires, I feel a marked tension: on the one hand, the idea of re-training as an immigration lawyer calls to me on the dimensions of meaning and impact. On the other hand, the idea of staying in AI calls to me on the dimensions of "importance," power, and influence, trying to shape the larger evolution of things in a positive way.

HORIZON

A LOST CAUSE

One of the most misleading and persistent tendencies of the mind is to attribute causation. We do this when we draw direct lines between one event and another and then base our further thinking on the assumption that this first event, prior in time, brought the second event or outcome into being. "I didn't get the job offer because of that awkward moment in the waiting room." Or, a little more complex, "I didn't get the offer because of that awkward moment in the waiting room and because of my hesitation with the first analytical problem that the interviewer put to me." In fact, it is quite possible that neither of these events even registered with the interviewer, who no doubt weighed many variables and impressions before coming to her final decision.

When we ask ourselves how we got to where we are in our current work or life situations, we usually make the mistake of thinking about a sequence of events that stretch from the past to our present condition. That is the first mistake. The second mistake is to then create a facile and rather simplistic story that explains how one thing followed and led to another. It seems that our psyches need the comfort of an explanation. Behind the first mistake is the fallacy that one moment of time has a causal relationship with the next moment in time. Causality is far more complex than what can be portrayed in even the most exhaustively detailed story. Behind the second mistake is the human need to take control of a situation, particularly a difficult situation, by having an explanation and producing a story that makes this whirring and buzzing world more comprehensible and therefore more predictable.

There is nothing wrong with a story that helps us understand our world a little bit better. What we need, however, is a *good* story, a better one than we usually make. When thinking about causation, Aristotle had a more elaborate tale to tell. He considered four forces that are always at play in the arising of any phenomenon or situation: the material cause, the formal cause, the efficient cause, and the final cause. Let us take, for example, the case of the first sprout of an oak tree emerging from the ground in the spring. The material cause is the nutrient substances available in the acorn. The efficient cause is interaction of soil, water, and sunlight under the right conditions that set the germination process in motion. The formal cause is the possibilities and constraints imposed by the material structure of the emerging plant in its particular setting in the soil.

The final cause is the one that dropped out of the popular imagination with the advent of "Enlightenment" thinking. Aristotle's final cause is what the acorn needs to become due to its very nature. In scientific parlance we would talk about the final cause as residing in the genetic structure of the acorn. More poetically, the future beckons: The acorn needs to unfold and become something that would be hard to discern from holding it in one's hand. Aristotle's word for this process was *telos*, often translated as *completion*: There is something that an acorn moves *toward*.

There wasn't much use for final cause as Newtonian physics took hold of common thinking in the seventeenth, eighteenth, and nineteenth centuries (and continues to this day in the popular imagination). It has made a reappearance, however, in the twentieth and twenty-first centuries on a number of fronts, in contemporary theoretical physics and in the work of thinkers such as Martin Heidegger, Carl Jung, Pierre Teilhard de Chardin, and Karl Rahner among many others. In the language of Heidegger and Rahner, we are beings who unfold. We have a sense of orientation toward something that is bigger than what we now sense ourselves to be, and we are in motion, need to be in motion, toward that something bigger. We feel most alive when we are walking toward it; we *need* to walk toward it.

In my work with my students and clients, I hear the language of final cause, the language of *Horizon*, with great frequency. "I like my work well enough, but lately I have started to think, "What's *next*?" "Where is all of this *going*?" "I used to be excited about work, where can I find that excitement now?" "It seems like I should be *further along* in my career." I often work with individuals who have a sense that something needs to be completed, that there should be a sense of journey or forward movement. This is all language that arises from a sense of walking toward something; it is *Horizon* language.

At times this language comes not from excitement but rather from a sense of inadequacy, self-judgement, and that all too human habit of comparisons with peers. All of these lead only to suffering. This sense of not having sufficiently "made it" is the evil twin of that deeper yearning toward more life whose energy propels our unfolding toward our own particular horizons. Making this discernment between the need to change for the sake of a fuller life and an anxious striving for more recognized accomplishment has been the theme of many of my coaching sessions. Here is the difference: Horizon *pulls* us, it is full of longing and beneath this longing, perhaps not yet felt, is excitement.

FIVE CHARACTERISTICS OF HORIZON

Horizon Is Bigger Than We Are

Horizon exerts a pull on us; it is compelling. We know that there is something larger than not just what we know but larger than what we *are* now, at this time. Try as we may, we cannot properly say what it is. We want to approach it because we want to be something bigger than we are now, we want to be more full and more alive. We want to know it by drawing nearer to it, but we are always sensing that there isn't a way that we can ever fully arrive, fully know it and "have" it.

Another way of saying this is that Horizon is not part of ego. Horizon is not part of what we call "me," it is not part of our "identity." It is something other than our talents, our intelligence, our accomplishments, our appearance, our preferences, or our personal history. The very turning toward Horizon places all of these things at our back as we step from them and out of them into a space that is unformed, uncertain, and open. We cannot sum up or give a good account of Horizon. It is always more than what we know and what we have already experienced.

Horizon Grows

As we walk toward our wanting for more life, Horizon accumulates. When we question deeply what is missing, when we experience yearning for greater participation in life, when we find activities and people and experiences that fill us, we are walking toward Horizon and accumulating more of it, more of its "more life," as we walk. We, of course, can avoid this journey if it feels too perilous. There are so many ways to stay in bed and pull the covers up over us. There are so many addictions that keep us from feeling deeply and acting in new ways. But if we venture forth, Horizon keeps its promise. We find ourselves inhabiting a more spacious sense of being. There is no less pain and no more pleasure, but there is more intensity and immediacy in our lives; we become more real. This continues if we keep on walking: Horizon grows within us even as it remains always in front of us.

We know this. Right now, checking inside, you can notice that you know more about what matters than what you knew ten years, five years, or even one year ago. If we remain open and curious, we learn about meaning and we do not forget. This learning gives us more being, makes us more real. It is not just about this, about our enlarged capacity to participate in life; it is also about a growing capacity to sense the next stretch of Horizon. We get better at this walking toward the next thing, which is always a new thing that will lead us into a larger world. If I asked you to plan a vacation right now that would be a rich experience, you would do a better job than you did three years ago. If I asked you if you would like to read this book, attend this play or movie, or even go to this party, you would do a better job of getting it right. Our instinct for meaning is a muscle that gets stronger with use.

Horizon Is Not a Goal

We cannot plot a course to Horizon. Anything that we would plot from our current mental model of the world could not be something new. We will never move closer to Horizon with a plan and a to-do list. And yet, in the high-achievement world that characterizes our global capitalist culture, I continually encounter those who want me to help them plan for more meaning: "Perhaps more yoga, more meditation, more travel, or a job change." Maybe, or maybe not.

When we are deeply moved by something that is truly new – a concert, or a painting, or a poem, or a personal loss, or a totally unanticipated experience – we realize that we have been changed by a force that comes from an unknown, and unknowable (by the analytical mind) place. We never could have arrived where we now find ourselves *by our own means*. The experience of Horizon is always a revelation to the analytical mind. We can cultivate our availability for experience at the Horizon (more on this later), but when it arrives, it always arrives from somewhere else, always arrives as a gift, and is always something new. Common advice from a Zen teacher to a student who is about to engage in *sesshin*, an intensive seven-day silent retreat, is "Expect nothing!" When Jesus was ready to enter Jerusalem for the culmination of his ministry on earth, he commanded a disciple to find, as transportation for this journey, "a colt that has never been ridden before." Experience of Horizon always comes on the back of a colt that has never been ridden before.

Horizon Is More Than Happiness

As I write this book, happiness and its measurement are quite in vogue among psychologists as well as the general public. Many books have appeared in the past decade or so about happiness and the paths that lead there. Happiness seems to be what people want. Among psychologists, the study of happiness is often referred to as "Hedonics." This word is taken from the Greek word for pleasure, and pleasure is what most people have in mind when they use the word. Happiness, as it is commonly understood, is a very pleasant emotional state. Horizon, on the other hand, is not a state. It is a path that includes the experience of many states as it is travelled.

The Horizon journey would be a diminished traveling if its destinations were the attainment of any one state. Clinging to that state, or a craving for more of it, would follow, and this clinging and craving would prevent us from being fully alive and open to whatever life has to offer us, and needs from us, next. This next reality might be quite challenging, but ultimately rewarding. Consider the journey of being a parent.

Consider the journey of a challenging vocation. The Horizon journey will include passages through times of happiness, but also through times of joy, grief, wonder, sorrow, and awe.

Horizon Is Intimate with Death

What is it that is out there that lies at the end of everything that we can imagine? We, as human beings, live with a sense of moving toward our ending. We wonder at this ending because its very nature evokes awe and mystery. We have our notions, our glimpses, we have the wisdom of our received traditions, but these are not the walking itself. This awe of what ultimately lies before us gives a sense of urgency and intensity to the journey. Horizon's pull to experience more life cannot be separated from our imagination of death. We want to get in as much as possible in the time that is given, we all want "to be written into the book of life." The mystery and lure of any horizon is the mystery of what lies beyond it. This twinship of Horizon and death, acknowledged or not, examined or unexamined, places existential energy behind the root question of Horizon: What does it mean, right now, to understand and move closer to life in its fullest?

THE DISTANCE TRAVELLED

In this section and the three sections that follow, we will be moving through exercises to find new language about our experience of Horizon. We will be looking to pick up *Horizon* from a place that is deeper than analytical intelligence, as we have with each of the three previous elements. We will, as before, start from a place of free attention and wait there with curiosity and energy to see what each of our questions calls forth. This return to free attention is, in itself, a profound turning toward Horizon. It requires us to rouse the energy necessary to let go of the thoughts, emotions, judgements, and conclusions that arise from our conditioned mind. It requires us to wait patiently with curiosity and energy at the frontier of our not-knowing. It asks that we drop all artifice and defense and face what arises just as it appears. It is just this open-hearted waiting without knowing, but with an excitement for what is not yet known, that sets the work of Horizon in motion. Our first question asks what we already know about Horizon. We will begin, as we did for roles, from a place of free attention. Please turn now to Appendix II to be guided into a place of free attention if you want to move through the exercise by reading the text itself. Alternatively, if you visit www.fourelementsbook.com , I will lead you through the process for using free attention and then step you through the exercise itself.

From this place of free attention, and not from your analytical mind, notice what images arise as you read the following sentence. Take your time and allow images to form and be replaced by new images. Do not be in a hurry to come to conclusions or to write. Rather, allow the images to gather in their own time. Here is the sentence:

"What do you already know about Horizon?"

In other words, what do you know about life in its fullest? What are the types of experiences that you cherish? The places? The people? What has been life-giving? What has not? Rather than current desires, situations, or merely pleasant occurrences or activities, what endures as being deeply important?

As your felt sense generates an image and that image itself becomes more stable, try to capture that image in a fresh sentence or a few fresh sentences. Pause after you are finished and return to the open awareness of your free attention and check for your felt sense and for whatever new images may be arising from it. Again, when the image becomes stable, try to capture it in a fresh new sentence or sentences. Remember, you are looking for what you know for sure about what it means to live life in its fullest.

Look at the sentences that you have written and underline the key words in each sentence. If the sentence seems fresh and if you feel it truly captures the essence of your felt sense, leave it. If the sentence still feels abstract, look at the key words and for each of the key words write a new sentence about what you really mean by that word. Do this for each of the sentences that seem abstract or stale.

HOW WE CARRY WHAT WE KNOW ABOUT HORIZON: PEOPLE

An important way that we understand Horizon is through role models. As we live and look around us we notice people who seem to embody the answer to the core Horizon question: What does it mean to live life in its fullest? I often ask my students, as they embark on an internship or post-graduation job, to notice who they begin to admire. I use the word "notice" deliberately. We do not arrive at role models through thinking. They simply arrive unbidden by our analytical mind. We notice that our admiration has been growing. When we recognize this, only then can we fruitfully employ analytical intelligence to help us go deeper: Why do we admire them? What do we really know about their desires and values? How did they get to the place where they are now such that they captured our attention and imagination?

Who, for you, provides an image of what it means to live life in its fullest? At different times in your life different people no doubt fulfilled this function. Over time, for all of us, certain people endure as living, or formerly living, symbols of what life is truly about. Most of us have several of these, but often there are two or three, or a few more, that stand above the others. This next exercise is designed to bring those people explicitly and exclusively to mind. The process must start from a place of free attention, so please turn now to Appendix II to begin. From that place of free attention, notice the answer that comes for the following question:

Who embodies what it means to live life in its fullest?

Be patient, as if you had cast your fishing line into the water and are waiting, all senses alert, for what may arrive. A name, or several names, may come very rapidly. Write those names down and return to your fisher-person's stance in free attention, waiting for other images and names to appear. Write the names down as they appear. When the new names that are arriving begin to be less compelling, stop and look at your list. Return to the place of your free attention as you read the list. Soak in it. If the list seems too long, pare it down to the few people that loom largest for you. Take each of the names that remain on your list in turn. From a place of free attention, write a few fresh sentences that answer the following questions: What is the essence of my admiration for this person? What aspect of life in its fullest do they teach me?

Read the sentences that you have written. Underline the key words in each sentence. If a sentence seems abstract or stale, write a fresh new sentence for what you want each key word to mean and include these new sentences as part of your response. When you have sentences that bring new and compelling language to what you have received from your most important role models, you have completed this part of the exercise.

HOW WE CARRY WHAT WE KNOW ABOUT HORIZON: TALISMANS

The great cathedrals are full of symbols: images in stained glass, stone, mosaics, tapestry, and bas relief that are far more than a means for conveying an edifying story. They carry something from an ancient tradition that is beyond the reach of the analytical mind. Something that is far more dense, nuanced, layered, rich, and polyvalent than a concept, idea, or piece of doctrine. The *symbolum* is a carrier of a human truth, and the truth of a lived tradition. The dizzying arch of the sheer vertical space is also a *symbolum*, as is the smell of incense and the prayers, chanting, and song that fill that space. The design of a cathedral, and its living activity, continually offer up talismans of what is ultimately most important. Everything about the cathedral points us toward Horizon, and points with things that we can see, touch, hear, smell, and, in the case of the taking of communion, taste.

A talisman is an object that represents a powerful and important force in our life. Indeed, etymologists point to the word's origin in the Greek word *telos*, which we have discussed above as pointing to fulfillment and completion. A talisman is a holder of fulfillment and meaning, and we human beings collect them whether we are aware of it or not. That special photo of a gathering of friends from ten years ago, grandmother's wedding ring, a lock of baby hair stashed away for years, tickets from a special night out with a special person, an overly worn sweater that has come to be the very manifestation of comfort and safety: talismans all.

A Horizon talisman is a particularly powerful object, book, poem, story, song, memory, place, activity, or experience, that has the ability, again and again, to remind us of what it means to live life in its fullest. By gazing at them, holding them, reading them (if only in part and briefly), listening to them, calling them to mind, and holding them in our attention, we are deeply reminded of what is most important.

Many of my most important talismans are books: the book on platonic dialog that took my most revered professor a lifetime to write; the *Philokalia*, which is a collection of the writing of spiritual masters from the Eastern Christian tradition; and certain poems by T.S. Eliot, Charles Williams, Rumi, Dante, Galway Kinnell, and others. Certain works of music such as Bach's B Minor Mass and certain songs of Leonard Cohen also have talismanic force for me. They serve to bring me back not to ideas, concepts, or moral principles but rather to what the pianist Glenn Gould called a "state of wonder" that attends upon my current participation in, and my emerging next steps toward, the Horizon experience.

A participant in one of my workshops on Horizon emailed

me to describe how, after the event, she retrieved an old worn and beautifully bound edition of the poems of Robert Burns that had been a talisman for her father and now, through her handling of it, a talisman of her own. She brought it into her office, where it could be within her gaze and close enough to pick up to handle and read when she needed to reset her compass bearing toward Horizon. This next exercise is designed to help you retrieve your most powerful talismans and, as this participant did, bring them back within easy reach so that you can use them, for talismans are meant to be *used*.

Read again the instructions given in the section above for letting go of your reliance on analytical mind and coming to a place of free attention. When you notice that you have become distracted, simply remove your attention from the train of thought that has captured you and return it to the core of your body. From that place of free attention, notice the answer that comes for the following question:

What are my touchstones, my talismans, that I can rely on to remind me and evoke anew for me what is most meaningful, most alive, and most beautiful in life?

Allow this question to arise into your free attention. Read it, or listen to it, as often as necessary. Pay attention to the images that are arising of the objects, books, poems, stories, songs, memories, places, activities, or experiences that come at the bidding of this question. You may be surprised by what arrives. As a particular image of a particular talisman arises, write it down and return to free attention and the question. Stay in this place of free attention with the question until meaningful images cease to arise.

THE HORIZON EXPERIENCE

The experience of Horizon is that of being at the very edge of everything that we feel that we know and have experienced. Fully alive there at the edge, waiting and alert, there is something out ahead. This something out ahead is not anything that we lack. Rather, what is out ahead is something that is exciting, exciting and beautiful. Beautiful even though unseen. What is it? We do not know, but there is a longing for it.

In what way does each person that came to you in the first exercise hold or represent something that is beautiful and exciting? Write a few sentences about what they represent to you. It is not the person that is important here, it is rather what they allow you to experience. They are just a reminder of something that it is exciting and beautiful that you want to move toward, something of *yours*, not something of theirs. What is it? Continue to write.

Pick up each of the talismans that came to you in the second exercise. One by one, hold each in your mind and turn it around in your mind's eye. As you do this, what does it put you in touch with? Each of the talismans conjure something important, unknown, exciting right there in front of you. The purpose of the talisman is to bring you this experience. Stay with this experience as long as possible. You can do this by entering the place of free attention and seeing how the experience with the talisman is right now for you and returning your attention to it. Rather than following some internal description or telling a story with your analytical mind, continue to stay with the experience itself by returning your attention to the center of your body.

When you're ready, begin to write a few sentences about what comes to you. This experience itself, the experience of waiting in intense free attention, is the experience of being at the Horizon. Only from this experience will you be able to learn, or rather discover, what things you can do next to have this very experience more and more. So continue to write, write about that which the talisman brings. If images come of things to do, people to connect with, or places to go that seem to be connected with the talisman, write a few sentences that describe them. Do not force it. If no images come, then your Horizon experience is, for now, just abiding in the state of free attention. Can you tolerate not knowing? Can you savor the excitement of just yearning for that which might come next and lead you into a larger space?

The point of trying to write about what you already know about Horizon, about the people that come to you that represent full life, or about the experience that comes when you consider each of your Horizon talismans, is not to capture or contain something. The point is to *have the experience* of being at the very outermost edge of your life right now looking outward, and facing that which is compelling and drawing you forward. The point of these exercises is to be able to abide, even for just a few minutes, at the very edge of your life and stand in the numinous experience of Horizon itself. It is from standing, or sitting, alert with anticipation, at this place that the first images or intimations of the next few steps forward may come. But do not expect them, do not demand anything of the experience of standing at the frontier of Horizon.

Instead, persist. Rouse the energy with your free attention to stay there and wait, with no expectations. This is an ancient human experience. This is the experience of the still hunter waiting at the edge of the open meadow at dawn, of sitting quietly in a cool, dark chapel, synagogue, or mosque before the music starts, of climbing on a trail not knowing what drew you to this mountain today but not needing to know, feeling deeply the excitement of moving upward. It is really only from this place that something truly new can come. It's from this place that some notion of what needs to happen next will appear. You've been at this place many times in your life. Looking back, you can remember those moments when you made what seemed like a small decision or took what seemed like a small turn and arrived at a place that, in retrospect, was the place that you needed to be, the place that brought something new into your life. So now, if words come, let them come. If words do not come, return to this place, this place of not knowing that is at the same time full of possibility. Experience as much as you can, and write if the words come.

There is a paradox in Horizon that plays out between our experience of it and our response to it. The experience is one of vastness, and opening possibility. Our response, as we try to move toward this possibility and actually make it real in our daily life, is accomplished only by small, immediate initiatives. We feel we must take action, but we find that we can only take action on a human scale. We must learn the grammar before we can speak the language and practice the scales before we can play the instrument. We try new behaviors in relatively safe settings. We can be bold but then have to stop and listen for where the boldness needs to go. The beauty of something new is found in the details of making it something real for us.

SOPHIE JENSEN

Horizon Deep Dive

1. What do you already know about Horizon?
Learning – in the sense-making, not textbook, way –
is the "what," "why," "how," and "outcome" of life.
Adventure expands my boundaries in both the inner
and outer worlds, delving into the unknown and taking on new challenges.
Beauty abounds in the natural world, from the small-
est stem of grass to the most majestic mountain.
Connection and *kindness* are what light up the dark
times.
One's life is like an *energy* circuit and some people,
places, and activities build energy while others de-
plete it. For me, deep *friendships*, trail running, and
travel bring the most energy.
Strength comes from *struggle* and its inherent opportunities (demands?) to build *resilience*. Strength:
personal *grit, integrity, wisdom* and *compassion*.
There will always be *surprises*; there is so much I
don't know in advance of how things are going to
evolve and unfold.
Stimulation leads to the most growth when it is diverse and *multi-faceted*, feeding my being on *intellectual, emotional, spiritual,* and *physical* levels
(rather than being unidimensional, such as having
stimulating work but no room for anything else).
Paying attention is what enables deep, transforma-
tive *reflection*.
Gratitude opens my eyes. Gratitude: *appreciating*
the sheer abundance of my good fortune, even
while making room for the things that are hard or

challenging or anxiety-provoking
It's my close *relationships* and my own *"being"* that truly mean the most to me and that I most want to nourish. Own "being": sense of *inner wellbeing* and self-care and connection.

2. Who embodies what it means to live life in its fullest?
Dad: I admire my dad's full *engagement* in life. His love of trail running drives both the exertion and renewal of much of his *energy*. He is also intensely engaged in his work, exploring the *history and evolution of our world* and helping *his students grow*. He is deeply *relational*, highly valuing family, friends and even new/temporary acquaintances, finding the *fun and humor* in many situations. Overall, he has taught me about "life in its fullest" on many dimensions from the first question of this Horizon Exercise – particularly around *being stimulated on multiple fronts*, namely in terms of his *passion for his work* and *trail running*.

My favorite poets: I admired the *intense "noticing"* of life that poets have and their capacity to capture something of life's *wonder, pain, and "aliveness"* in their writing. They seem to pay close attention to the *world around and within them* and to *reflect deeply and creatively* on what they see. They appear to me in some ways as *"students of life"* who have, through their poems, much to offer others who want to learn through their writing. Overall, my favorite poets have taught me about "life in its fullest" on the dimension of *meaning/sense-making*, emphasizing the roles of paying attention and *growing through struggle*.

3. What are my touchstones, my talismans, that I can rely on to remind me and evoke anew for me what is most important, most alive, and most beautiful in life?
1. Book of my favorite poems
2. Pictures of the Pacific Northwest's natural beauty
3. Alumni holiday card
4. Various inspirational quotes that I return to
5. Samantha's card
6. Vivaldi's Four Seasons
7. Dancing
8. Trail running, especially in the Cascade mountains.
9. University of Chicago campus
10. The ocean

4. In what way does each person that came to you in the earlier exercise hold or represent something that is beautiful and exciting?
Dad: Dad represents adventure and physical exertion. He also represents full engagement in meaningful work, simultaneously engaging fully in his non-work life; he gets energy from his trail running and both uses that energy and gets more from his work. When I think of my dad, I think of humor, energy, fun, and exploration.

My favorite poets: These poets represent the ability to live and share the beauty and fragility of life and the world around us. They represent the opportunity to dig into the core of one's being and experiences and distill something beautiful and moving.

5. What do each of the talismans that came to you earlier put you in touch with?

1. Book of my favorite poems: Calm, creativity, beauty, finding meaning in grief/sadness. *Images: exploring*

2. Pictures of Pacific Northwest natural beauty: Beauty, nature, space, clarity, pristine-ness, time, stillness, stepping back to the bigger view, connectedness/ roots, identity, wonder, summer, family. *Images: running, kayaking, camping, water, solitude*

3. Alumni holiday card: community, learning, aspiration, excellence. *Images: professors, close college friends, campus, teaching*

4. Various inspirational quotes that I return to: energy, meaning, inspiration, seeking and speaking one's own truth. *Images: reading, philosophy*

5. Samantha's card: celebration, energy, authenticity, "true north" compass, own brand of "leadership," excitement, aliveness, sense of thriving. *Images: . . . ?*

6. Vivaldi's Four Seasons: energy, conviction, beauty, peace in movement. *Images: engaging*

7. Dancing: *energy, excitement, flow, instinct, joy, laughter, exuberance. Images: dance classes, music, running*

8. Trail running, especially in the Cascade mountains: space, time, stillness, quiet, beauty, adventure, perspective, joy, gratitude. *Images: lake, mountains, breathing. Close friends and family*

9. University of Chicago campus: stimulation, community, meaning, exploration, learning, surprises, friendships, sense of self. *Images: talks/lectures, fitness*

10. The ocean: breadth, depth, space, movement, bigness, freshness, horizon (literally and figuratively!). *Images: water, walks, fresh air, breathing, meditating.*

THE HORIZON PARADOX: GUIDING STARS AND THE NEXT SMALL STEP

There is a paradox at work in the heart of the Horizon arche-type. On the one hand, the Horizon experience seems formed by the thousand-foot gaze toward aspirations, values, and role models that have come to us from many sources in ways that we understand and in ways that we don't. On the other hand, the work of Horizon can only be accomplished in the here and now. Our images and symbols of Horizon may seem like guiding stars in the impeccably clear desert night sky; our role models, touchstones, and peak experiences may imbue and revive us with a sense of direction, but the Horizon journey is always just the next step we must take down here on earth.

My students and participants in my workshops, often action-ori-ented business people, are typically eager to get to the "action plan." So what do we do with this? What we do at first is often difficult for those of us who have been conditioned to feel most comfortable with clear goals and a clear path to the rewards for getting there. What we do first is spend a bit more time learning from Horizon. We need to feel the pull of what is most important. We think that we need to solve our problems before we can live our lives, but that will never get us there. It will only lead to a Hamlet-like sense of living a life of abstraction and delay. Rather, we must step into the full experience of our immediate situation, as discomforting as it may be. The way forward must be lived rather than solved.

Roger Torrey was a participant in one of my workshops who was crafting, with the help of his small group, his "career and life criteria," ten to twelve sentences that each capture a dimension of essential meaning. In his early sixties, Roger was in the process of selling the family business after several decades in the role of CEO. The business had been in the family for generations, so this was a momentous time indeed. Roger knew that one of his goals, one of his career and life criteria, had to be concerned with his growing pull to spend more time with his family. Initially, Roger's writing was rather abstract: "I need to spend more quality time with my family." As he spent time in the workshop going to the frontier of where his life now was, he was, more and more, able to write specifically about was what was pulling him in regard to his family relationships. He was eventually able to craft the following sentence: "I need to make dedicated time to be alone with my daughter, her husband, and child without any expectations."

His words are very particular. They are fresh and new and they were able to tell him something that he knew implicitly, but for which he had no language. Sitting there in free attention, at a time when he sensed deeply that a major part of his life frontier had shifted from the realm of work to the realm of family, he waited to see what would arise.

His final sentence is full of Horizon language; it is about being fully present with no expectations. It is also particular and actionable. What he felt pulling him turned out to be what seems a small and simple gesture: an overture to his daughter to be with her in a specific way. But isn't this the way that life so often invites us forward, asking us to make small gestures that bring us just that much closer to what really matters? Retirement and leaving what have been the major efforts and environments of our working world, when seen from a distance, would seem to be one of life's major upheavals. We cannot live, however, in the grand sweep of things, nor do we live in the plans that we generate in the face of big life changes.

We live in this day, in this moment, and are continually building our new life like a bird fashions her nest, adding and subtracting a twig here and there. Real life is lived in the built environment of these small affirmative movements. We need to release life of the burden of offering us something grand. Our Horizon is more vast than the grandiose construction of what we think we want, what we see others having, what appears to be important. We need to allow it to be vast, allow ourselves not to know, and allow ourselves to take the next small step into it.

CARRYING FORWARD

Now if a bird or a fish tries to reach the end of its element (sky or water) before moving in it, this bird or this fish will not find its way or its place . . .

- From Eihei Dogen's *Genjo Koan*
Translated by Robert Aitken and Kazuaki Tanahashi

It is only human to want to know how it all ends, to catapult to a solution with certainty and comfort. We believe that we need to meet life armored with a strategy and an action plan. We think that we need to solve our problems before we can live our lives, but that will never get us there. It will only lead, as Dogen suggests, to confusion and a sense of losing our way. Rather, we must begin to swim or fly; we must step into the full experience of our lives as they are right now. The problem is resolved in the living of the solution.

Cassie Sundstrom was a partner at a successful management consulting firm. She had also cultivated a lifelong interest in healthcare policy, and in particular healthcare delivery in developing nations. Her healthcare work had largely been pro bono, flying to various developing nations and working with healthcare agencies as they attempted to build out healthcare systems with their limited resources. She had become a respected expert in this area. Cassie is a hard worker. Between a consulting job and the several trips she took to far-flung places each year, she found herself questioning how all of this could be sustainable with her two middle school children whom she was raising largely on her own after a recent divorce. On top of all this, she wrote articles on healthcare policy and taught a healthcare policy class at a local university. The teaching had become a particularly strong passion for her in recent years.

Cassie came to see me when a position in the healthcare area opened up at the university. She applied for the position just to see what would happen, but was secretly harboring a growing sense of excitement. She had just recently been told that she was, indeed, on the shortlist for the job. This news brought with it a crisis. Her role at the consulting firm was highly remunerative and, should the job offer come through, the teaching position would pay about half of her current income. For the first time an opportunity was right in front of her to make her deepest interest the center of her working life. At the same time, Cassie is a dedicated mother who realized clearly her financial obligations to her family. She was at an impasse.

Stories that stretched into the future would form for Cassie. In one story, she accepted the teaching position and was able to develop her course further and new ones as well. She would have more time for her writing and more time for her healthcare consulting travel. In this scenario, she and her children would be living on a reduced budget. Also, there was no guarantee that this position would lead to tenure; she would have to work hard in terms of both writing and networking to make that happen. In the other story, she remained at the consulting firm, which, in fact, she genuinely enjoyed, and continued to earn a very good salary while keeping the momentum of her highly recognized and respected career. She would continue to travel on a limited basis to do her healthcare work. Our lives cannot carry forward in abstraction, in the realm of analytical thought alone. Cassie saw this clearly and realized that she would have to live her answer and create her next work life reality. She sat again and again in free attention as each of the four elemental archetypes, Identity, Necessity, Community, and Horizon, made their current reality and requirements known to her. Cassie, a meditation teacher herself, did this well.

Cassie was doing what we all do when we find ourselves on a fork in the road of life. She was looking down each of the forks as far as she could see, and then constructing a story about what lay behind the bend in both of those directions. At some point, however, as for all of us, the road of the mental construction itself runs out . . . and what about that other road, that road not taken? Where might it go and what would it look like, say, five years from now? And, a question that is put before me quite often, could she ever switch back? If she takes one road could she ever get back to the other fork once having traveled? Cassie put these questions before me right after she did indeed receive the teaching job offer. Sitting across from her in my office, I paused and gave my answer: "You cannot know. There is no way for you to know."

Although Cassie turned down the job offer, a path showed itself that would allow her to increase her focus on teaching. Several months later, after making her decision, Cassie wrote me a thank you note. In that note she said that that particular response from me, "You cannot know," was probably the most helpful interaction of our time together. It brought her a sense of relief and freed her for a different approach. When we no longer try to escape our sense of being lost and uncertain, but rather turn toward it and stay with it, we become aware that there is that within us that is already opening to something for which there are no words and which does not fall into any of the categories and labels that we had placed on it.

More and more, as our trust in life itself grows, we learn to give ourselves permission to not know and to be boldly curious and inquisitive at the very edge of where our not-knowing is leading. It is from this place alone that something truly new, something new that is always already there, can come to be real in our lives. The practice of free attention is what allows us to stay at this growing edge of our lives. More and more, we can develop the capacity to remain in free attention at the very edge of whatever is emerging, as uncomfortable as it might be, in the realms of Identity, Community, Necessity, and Horizon. Using free attention within the framework of the Four Elements, and doing exercises such as the *Integration for Intentions* exercise in this chapter, are not ways to understand and prepare for a future decision; they are the first acts of living in our new reality.

AN INTEGRATION FOR INTENTIONS

The purpose of this exercise is to place before your awareness your total experience, at this moment in time, of your work with each of the Four Elements. It is ephemeral: It is a way of presenting, symbolically, the forces of all four of the elements at play in your life at this time only. Even one month from now, the language that you produce in doing this exercise may be notably different. This exercise is not an attempt to "wrap things up." It is, rather, intended as a potent reminder of what would, indeed, *open* things up by pointing to what is most important as you take your next steps forward. We will begin, as always, from a place of free attention. Please turn now to Appendix II to be guided into a place of free attention if you want to move through the exercise by reading the text itself. Alternatively, if you visit www.fourelementsbook.com, I will lead you through the process for using free attention and then step you through the exercise itself.

Set aside at least an hour during which you will not be interrupted. Slowly and carefully, read through what you have written in response to each of the Four Elements exercises. Deliberately, change your posture and move into a place of free attention. Allow the words that you have been reading to work on you. Soak in them. When you become distracted or when your analytical mind wants to come to a premature conclusion, simply return your attention to your foundation of mindfulness as you would do during any episode of free attention practice.

Continue to do the work of staying in a place of free

attention. When you are ready, take each of the Four Elements in turn, beginning with Identity. For each of the elements, write two or three declarative sentences. Begin each sentence with a phrase that indicates intentionality, for example: "I will . . ."; " I want . . ."; or " I need . . ." After reading each sentence, pause and return to a place of free attention. How does that sentence resonate? Is it alive, specific, and authentic? If it feels too abstract, go back to the sentence and replace the word or words that feel too abstract with words that are more lively and specific. Your sentence is complete when, by reading it, you know, in the center of your body, that you have a handle on something that is vital for the decision that you face. When you are ready, go on to the next sentence. When you have finished at least two sentences for the Identity element, move on to Community. Repeat this process for the Community, Necessity, and Horizon elements.

This exercise allows you to move from an implicit sense of your work with all four of the elements to a symbolic representation of what you have learned about how these psychological forces are now affecting your life. The sentences that you produce can themselves now be used as "touchstones" as you move through the decisions that you currently face. Most of them will not be as durable as the touchstones that you identified during your work on the Horizon element; they are for now. A sample is provided to give you a sense of the outcome of this exercise.

Four Elements Integration for Intentions

Identity

- I am a manger and want a role leading a team of direct reports
- My role needs to clearly identify me as a digital marketing professional
- My next position must require and reward my skill as an inspiring public presenter

Community

- I want to work for an organization that is highly effective and growing substantially
- I want to work for an organization where communication is fluid and senior managers are highly accessible
- I want to work for an organization that is highly relational, where co-workers typically develop friendships

Necessity

- Due to my parents' age and health issues, it is vital that we remain in the Chicago area
- With college tuition for both of our children rapidly approaching, it is important that I make at least $95,000
- Given that my relationship with my son revolves around his commitment to athletics, I need to be free to attend the majority of his weekend games

Horizon

- I want to honor the commitment that I have made to our church council over the next three years
- I need to protect half an hour every morning to

deepen my meditation practice
- I want to continue our family tradition of protecting the time for at least one week every year together in an inspirational natural environment

APPENDIX I

DECISION-MAKING USING THE PHILOSOPHY OF THE IMPLICIT

Our contemporary global capitalist culture teaches and rewards analytical problem-solving above all other types of intelligence. Within this culture the word "smart" more often than not refers to a person's capacity for analytical thought. However, decisions like those that Sophie was facing are decisions that require the full self: Should I live here? Should I marry this person? Should I take this job? These decisions, especially when several are being asked at the same time, can't proceed from analytical intelligence. Analytical intelligence always functions from our current mental model based on our previous experience, and it is the narrowness of this model itself that prevents us from seeing what is important and new. For what needed to happen in Sophie's life was something new, something that she hadn't lived before.

There are other types of human intelligence that *do* allow us to encounter and take hold of what has never been in our experience or current mental model. They also allow us to problem-solve within the context of our whole life situation. These types of intelligence are less recognized and rarely taught in the current global culture, but they can be learned and deliberately cultivated. They are the cognitive paths to the something new that is required when we must step into what our lives, in all of their complexity, now require. I would like you to have the actual experience of contrasting analytical and non-analytical intelligence. To do this, I will as two questions.

Two Questions

For each question, I ask that you do two things. The first thing that I ask is that you genuinely try to answer the question. I want you to come up with an answer, the best answer that you can find. The second thing that I ask is that while you are trying to answer the question, you observe your own process. We all have this capacity to use our free attention to watch, in a non-analytical and non-judgmental way, our own process. In this case, you will be looking with your free attention at the way in which you are finding your answer. Even more specifically, I want you to notice *where in your body* you are looking for your answer.

Here is the first question: What is the square root of 22? Try as hard as you can to find an answer to one decimal place. Take your time, but as you are trying to answer, notice where your attention is focused, notice what part of your body you are using for your search for an answer and notice where your attention is. What is the square root of 22? Where in your body is the answer coming from? Note your answer to both of these questions and only then move onto the next paragraph.

Here is the second question: Why did you *really* buy this book? What compelled you to pick it up and start reading? What about your life wanted you to read this book? These are all variations on the question being asked. Try hard to answer the question truly. What are you looking for from this book? As you try to answer that question, look at how you are answering it. Where in your body are you looking for the answer? When you have an answer to both of these questions, move on to the next paragraph.

I have asked these two questions, or slight variations on them, in many settings, and to people from over seventy nations. After asking the first question, the square root of 22, or, sometimes, the distance from Cambridge to Beijing in kilometers, I ask the second part of the question, "Where in your body did you look for the answer?" Regardless of venue or national culture, more than 90 percent of the people in the room will indicate that they looked for this answer in their head, (they typically answer by pointing toward their heads).

I then ask my second question, which for my audiences often takes the form of "Why did you come here? Why did you *really* come here?" I give them a minute or so to formulate their answer. I tell them that I want a real answer, their best effort. I tell them that I want a thirty-second authentic statement concerning their deepest motives, hopes, wishes, and expectations.

I then ask the second part of the question, "Where in the body did you look for your answer?" This time, some people point to their lower abdomen, their "gut." Others point to their solar plexus or to the area around their heart or to their throat. I then ask for a show of hands for how many experienced their looking as occurring somewhere below the chin. More than 90 percent raise their hands.

Intelligence as a Way of Knowing

What is going on here? Most people associate the act of thinking with the brain, and most people locate this brain that does the thinking as occupying the space within the cranium. Yet clearly we think with different parts of our body, and, more amazingly, we use different parts of our body to answer different types of questions. What we loosely call thinking is a misnomer. Different things are going on, using different parts of the self, when we look for the answers to different types of questions.

My two questions were designed to deliberately evoke two very different types of cognition. The first question, a request for mathematical computation, calls for what I will refer to as analytical intelligence. Analytical intelligence is itself multiple, with mathematical computation being one variety. This is a question of a type that sounds familiar to us all. This type of question has echoed in our classrooms through recent centuries. "Compare and contrast the motivations for and patterns of English and Spanish colonial acquisitions in the sixteenth and seventeenth centuries" is another, non-mathematical, type of question that calls on analytical intelligence.

Most—I am tempted to say all—of the students in my classes at Harvard have been rewarded, since kindergarten, primarily for the facility of their analytical intelligence. I can make this same statement about the students at the many universities at which I have lectured throughout the United States and around the world. It seems to be what counts the most when it comes to school admission and evaluation of performance.

My second question, however, asked my audience to *look for meaning* and to *represent meaning*. At times of transition in life and work it is precisely the search for meaning and our ability to describe it that are called for. Analytical intelligence will become important at a latter point in the process, but we can't *start* there. As we shall see, nothing *new* can come from

143

analytical intelligence. We must begin with two very different ways of knowing.

You Are an Implicit Intricacy

When I asked you the second question, "Why did you *really* buy this book," you began a search. You knew an answer was there (after all, you are reading the book.) But the question asked you to go deeper, to be more precise, to ask yourself again, to discard any top-of-mind response. Why are you *really* reading the book? Why did you *really* marry your spouse? Why did you *really* leave your job? Yes, the answer is indeed there, but that answer is intricate. So many things are interacting with each other, affecting each other to produce a decision and an action.

There is always more to intricacy than what has been defined or can be defined. For example, let's look at your choice to be with your spouse or partner. This could involve many different aspects of your relationship with your mother, your father, or your older sister. It might involve your sister's choice for a partner as well. It involves what you experienced and learned, consciously and unconsciously, from every other romantic relationship up to the time of your choice. The serendipity, the mood, the events earlier that day before your first date are also interacting. Your feelings or beliefs, conditioned in ways that are mostly outside your awareness, about a life alone or in relationship are playing their part. Your partner is physically attractive to you in a way that has also been conditioned in subtle and not so subtle ways by past experience. His or her values also largely resonate with yours, but how did yours form? Consider the vast array of experiences and interactions that operate to inform how your life priorities, right now, sort themselves out. And yet they are a *whole*.

The list of everything that interacts to form our experience of the present moment with all of its circumstances and contingencies goes on and on. It is a list without end that, with infinite time and infinite precision, would describe an exquisitely complex network of experiences, conditions, beliefs, thoughts, feelings, and environmental realities. The psychologist Eugene Gendlin refers to this complex network as an *implicit intricacy*. He points out that all of the elements of this network affect *each other* and change each other (Gendlin's terms are *inter-affecting of everything by everything*) as they form the intricate ever-changing matrix from which choice and action emerge.

Carrying Forward

All of this inter-affecting seeks expression in our actual behavior, in what actually needs to happen for us next. Right now, remember a time when you had to make a decision. A decision that may not have been extremely consequential, but, on the other hand, was not simple either. Let us say that it is at the end of the day on Friday and you are sitting at your desk at work. It has been a long week and a long workday. Your plans for the weekend have been vaguely forming in the background. There are several things that you want to do, and you will not have time for all of them. There's a part of you that wants to get outdoors and walk. There's a part of you that wants to make plans to meet friends tomorrow. You have been beginning to think about the evenings and the best way to use them. And then the telephone rings.

It is an old friend, someone you have not seen in quite some time, and he's calling to invite you to an impromptu dinner party on Saturday night. You are surprised by the call and pleased to hear his voice. But all at once your thoughts and feelings about the weekend have been turned on end. You thank him for the invitation and tell him you'll need to get back later on in the evening because you need to check on other commitments.

This type of situation occurs for all of us on a regular basis. What do you do now? Perhaps right after putting your phone down, you sit very still in your chair. Or maybe you get up and walk over to the window or step outside to walk around the block. What is going on? On the surface, it would seem that what is going on is quite simple: do you want to go to that dinner party or not? But really, so much more is involved.

The real question that cannot be avoided is: What needs to happen right now? Now, and throughout this weekend, what most needs to emerge in your life? What is most important? How do you find out what is most important? How can you be sure? What are your needs? What are you desires? What do you want to avoid?

These are questions that fall into the implicit background during most of your waking hours. When you are involved in activities that require your attention and your immediate efforts, these implicit questions, always there, do not become explicit. But now, catalyzed by a brief telephone call, the questions are before you. As you sit there in your chair, quite still now, what exactly are you doing? You are engaging a very particular type of human intelligence. Some might call it "looking for your gut feel" and others might call it "using intuition," but really it is something else, something much more precise. You are allowing all of the claims on your life, all of the claims on your being, to be present and to function completely in an open space where there is not yet an answer, where there is not yet knowing. Your very attention in the still sitting heats up the interaction of these seemingly contradictory wishes, hopes, and fears. And in the middle of it all, the question is there: What do I want to do? What do I need to do? What does life need now?

You come to an answer. Your state of bodily tension, the frustration of not knowing, and the press of a deadline shift. There is a sense of release. No, you do not want to be at that dinner party; you really do want to see that movie whose reviews have intrigued you. You will graciously decline. The answer is always first in the body. It is a "body feel" for what is needed, even before you are able to describe it. There was, from the very beginning, no "rational" answer to be had. There was no way that your analysis, in the abstract, could assign priority or weightings to all the different possibilities for this weekend. But there was another process, a different human way of knowing. Conscious of it or not, you engaged in a process that allowed you, after considerable effort of attention and turning things over, to come to a sense of what needed to happen next.

Your presence or absence at a dinner party, and what you might give up in order to be in attendance, are rather small stakes. But that call might have been about another matter altogether. It might have been a call announcing great loss, or a real threat to your life situation. Or that call might have brought a great joy that seemed to change everything and, seemingly all at once, opened up new possibilities that will also require choice and decision. Or you might find yourself at a major juncture at work where your decision feels weighty indeed. In these cases, you would have to sit still again, or take that walk around the block, and pay the same type of intense attention (because you cannot simultaneously *think* about it *all*) to how everything in your life and personal history affects everything else. You would have to hold this intense attention to uncover what this news means for how all those different parts of your being. We may be, as Walt Whitman expressed it, a "multitude" of selves, but with everything that that call changed, your life *as a whole* must now be carried forward in a new direction, into these new possibilities.

This *carrying forward*, for us human beings, is not automatic. It requires the recognition that something new is implied and an effort to move into what this something new might be. It is like the urgency that the hermit crab feels when his borrowed shell is starting to feel tight again and he must abandon it for a larger home or . . . he will die. We carry forward not just to get along, but to inhabit a larger world. We are moved to inhabit a world that cannot even be described by our current understanding, our current language. This movement comes from our implicit intricacy seeking to become even more intricate, larger, more spacious.

Much like that hermit crab, that old job was starting to feel tight, in ways that took us quite a while, perhaps, to understand. Any attempt to describe what we needed at the first feelings of tightness would have failed. We would have been attempting (as we almost always do) to use old language and old images to describe a land that we had not yet entered. Our thinking and problem-solving at times of inflection tries to re-arrange thoughts and images of how we were, how we are, and how the world works into some picture of how things could be better. This never works, for a simple reason: These images and thoughts concern a world that no longer exists.

A Poverty of Wonder

Gendlin's model questions the model of the universe as a vast set of billiard balls set in motion in time and space and colliding with all of their consequent effects. Life is not a rearrangement of the same unchanging units in a different pattern. Gendlin would say that we, and our environment, are already being changed by the circumstances that demand our response. The new "solution" cannot be determined by the rearrangement of the old units. We must pay attention, for something new is, in fact, already happening. This does not deny what seems to us to be a sequence of cause and effect, but rather draws our attention to the amazing implicit intricacy of these causes and effects. This intricacy cannot be reduced to the relationship of separate units that remain more or less the same as they interact, like those billiard balls. Something truly *new* cannot arise from a remixing of the same ingredients. For this reason, something truly new cannot be apprehended by thinking about it with what we already know.

And yet we keep on trying to make the present, let alone what is emerging as the future, just another version or rearrangement of the past. We do this all the time. I put on the clothes that the night before I imagined I would wear, only to arrive at work and realize that it is much colder today. I walk into the kitchen in the morning and begin to pour the same cereal, my supposed favorite, into the familiar bowl, adding raisins because that taste has worked well in the past. But this morning has never come before. If I were to pay attention, I might notice that I am hungry in a different way this morning. If I were to stop and drop my conditioned model of breakfast-making and truly pay attention to my full awareness, to try to hold a felt sense of my hunger, I might discover this "different type of hunger" was something like "more hungry" or "wanting a feel of being more full." I might realize then that I want more protein and with that, search to see if there are eggs in the refrigerator. Or maybe I would not pay attention and eat the cereal and then realize, on the drive to work, that I am still very hungry.

When I arrive at work, I expect to have one sort of conversation about familiar topics with Jeremy and another type of conversation altogether with Billie because my relationship with Billie has developed in a certain way and I know her less well than I know Jeremy. I have my "talking with Jeremy" model and my "talking with Billie" model. But Billie is different today, she is trying to connect with me about something very important but I do not realize this until after she has left my office. Right after she leaves, I have a funny sensation as if something is amiss but I am not sure what. If I am busy, I might try to ignore it, shrug it off. If I were to really focus my awareness on this sensation and follow it, I might arrive at something like, "I was doing my Billie type conversation, but she was not doing her Billie conversation. What she was saying about her daughter really shook her and she was saying something new, looking for new way to talk with me. I did not know this and persisted in my model of 'talking with Billie.' The felt sense of the "funny sensation" is a signal from my implicit understanding of all of this; my talking with Billie now needs to become something different. Next time I see her, I must start over, paying close attention and making no assumptions about the conditions and the rules of our relationship.

Is something new possible at all? Again and again, we find ourselves in situations, be it in relationships or in problem-solving, where we persist in applying our conditioned mental models even when faced with evidence that they do not work. Often in a psychotherapy or coaching session I realize that I am listening to my client applying his or her model over and over again and being unwilling to accept the fact that the model isn't working. Dropping a model that has worked in the past, being willing to truly see into how we are responding in a conditioned way, is a difficult thing. We so cherish our certainties; we cling to the past. The poet Rainer Maria Rilke said that he yearned to "live in the un-interpreted world"; he wanted to live in a full and immediate awareness of things themselves, whatever they might be, rather than continually interpreting or "modeling" his experience.

Check now to see what you actually believe about all of this. Be curious and take your time; don't jump to conclusions. Do you seem to assume that each day is indeed different, but this difference is essentially a rearrangement of the same "stuff" as yesterday, only a little bit colder, less sunny, and with more wind? And when you meet your colleague on the stairs at work in the morning, is he the same "unit" as yesterday, but now moving quickly because he is late rather than standing and waving, in a different set of clothes, as when you left him yesterday? Or does it seem that your assumption is that of stepping into a very different world each day? Our beliefs determine what we perceive and therefore the boundaries of what is possible.

The Secret Is in the Sequence

Analytical intelligence, the intelligence of building models, consciously or not, for pattern recognition, is a powerful human capacity, but it is a capacity that looks at an already existing order. We put the data in the spreadsheet, apply the tried and true algorithms, and interpret the rearranged results for a "result" upon which we base our action plan. But where did those algorithms come from? When real life, "the data," is new and the algorithms no longer take into account the ways in which the world around us has shifted, then we are looking at our lives through yesterday's eyes. If something new is to happen for us, it must begin with a way of "having," of taking hold of so that we can use and participate in what is being implied by the full intricacy of our whole, immediate life situation before we categorize or analyze it. Human beings have this capacity to take in the whole of their immediate situation, and all at once. I refer to this type of cognition as *implicit intelligence.*

The second step is to bring what we know implicitly into the full knowing that comes only when we create fresh new language that captures our new and emerging experience (Gendlin's term is *explication*). I call this type of knowing *symbolic intelligence.* Only after we have had a direct connection with what we know implicitly and bring this connection into new language can we use analytical intelligence to plan and act on what we have discovered. The secret is in the sequence: implicit knowing becoming symbolic clarity becoming analysis for action. In our current culture, implicit and symbolic intelligence are rarely taught and cultivated. This has left us with a poverty of wonder. It has made us far more vulnerable to boredom, alienation, addiction, and a sense of powerlessness. It has inured us to a sense of sameness, repetition, and inevitability. Do only the poets escape?

Implicit Intelligence
Step One: The Open Field of Free Attention (Making Space for the Necessary New)

Being true to life means being completely available. The world asks us to meet it, to offer a deliberate conscious gesture to receive what is offered, what is new. If we do not make this gesture, our lives continue on automatic pilot, being driven by our history of conditioning. We head toward the café because our conditioning is signaling "caffeine." Perhaps we begin to pick up our pace because the glance at the clock elicits the unnoticed cognition that we are late. The idea of being late, even if not recognized, is conditioned with an emotional element of fear of shame: if we arrive late to the meeting, we will be embarrassed. So, without the mediation of thought, there is now more adrenaline and cortisol in our blood and we are indeed moving more rapidly through the house and toward the door. Conditioning is multi-layered and intricate; it is also almost completely unconscious. Is it possible to be free of conditioning? What would this mean? What is this gesture, this necessary effort, that would allow us to be true to life, to respond to life in a completely available, spontaneous, unconditioned way?

We cannot think our way out of conditioning. That would be like pulling ourselves out of the mud by grabbing hold of our heels: Our thinking itself is conditioned. Human beings, however, have another type of intelligence at their disposal that has the capacity, if only temporarily, for unconditioned seeing. We have a capacity to self-observe, not in the sense of thinking about ourselves but in the sense of a deliberately held open awareness of our ongoing experiencing. If we remember to do so and "wake up," we can observe our own process without the interference of thinking about it. This awareness is an open field in that the awareness itself is like a dynamic energized field in which the contents of our conditioned (automatic) thoughts, emotions, associations, memories, judgements, urges, and images come and go.

Creating this open field, and developing our capacity to do so, is the necessary first step for cultivating implicit intelligence. It also allows us to see just how mechanical we really are and how we hold the possibility of something new at bay by placing our automatic judgements and assumptions on any spontaneously arising experience. The effort to use free attention unmasks our artificial, and defensive, restriction of the universe. The deliberate act of *free attention* allows us to remove these restrictions and experience life as it is actually happening. Without fee attention, there is no real ability to choose a new direction or behavior. Free attention can be learned.

- We can break the process of free attention into its elements:
- The decision to focus attention directly in the middle of the body
- The arising of conditioned patterns of thoughts and emotions
- The suspension of the analytic response
- Making the choice and effort to give energy to pure attention rather than the arising thoughts and emotions
- Returning the attention to the body each time we find ourselves caught in associations and storylines
- Let's try it right now.

Sit in a chair with a comfortable but upright posture. Direct your attention to the middle of your torso, anywhere from your throat to your lower abdomen. Allow your free attention to rest there. Notice that keeping your attention requires an effort. As you try to do so, you become aware of the conditioned thoughts, memories, and images, and the emotions that come with them spontaneously arise. This is not your "thinking"; it is mechanical, automatic. If, instead of returning your attention to the sensation in the middle of your body, you give attention to the stream of thoughts, feelings, and associations, they will become a storyline, and there will be a judgement, "This is good, this is bad, this is just neutral." You now have competition for your awareness and what you were doing with it.

Allow the emerging thoughts and emotions to follow their own course but do not feed them with your attention, imagination, or will. Do not allow images to become a string of associations that in turn become a storyline by feeding them with your attention. The trick is to see it happening and at that very point to redirect your attention to the sensation in the middle of your body. If you wish, you may return your attention to the palm of your right hand as your "foundation of mindfulness." For some people, returning their attention to the breath works best. Make a choice: center of the body, palm of the right hand, or breath, but once you make a choice stick with it.

Have no expectations as you return your attention to your foundation of mindfulness (the middle of your body, the palm of your right hand, your breath). Allow your attention to rest there, giving your attention to the bodily sensation and the energy that it needs so as not to be caught up in the string of thoughts, emotions, associations, and judgements. Have an open and curious mind. Do not expect anything. Suspend the need of your analytical mind to figure out what is happening or to impose any type of order or understanding onto your experience. Suspend your need, the need of your conditioned analytical mind to know, to have a sense of where things are going, or to have a sense of whether or not this whole endeavor is worth it.

This experience of free attention will be a threat, in fact, to that part of you that needs to know, that needs to pin things down, that needs to get somewhere. Continue to get nowhere, continue not to know. Continue to return your attention to your foundation of mindfulness. Continue to allow whatever needs to arrive to arrive. At first, it may seem as if nothing is happening, and your "inner critic" will tell you that this is exactly so and that you are wasting your time. Whenever the inner critic appears, a good strategy is to simply smile. Do not allow your inner critic or your judging mind to interfere with your open awareness anchored in your foundation of mindfulness. Simply return your attention, again and again, to your foundation of mindfulness in the body.

This practice of free attention is, in many ways, like pressing the "reset button" of our intention and awareness. When we rouse the intention and energy that implicit cognition requires of us and engage in the act of pure presence, and make the choice to remain in that process, we are allowing everything that is able to function in our life to function. We are allowing everything that needs to emerge, that wants to be lived, to emerge. We are leaving nothing out. Anything that has been exiled, because it was too painful, sad, angry, or threatening in any other way, is now allowed to show itself. We do not engage in "short-circuiting" of our field of awareness through various addictions or subterfuges. We do not grab our smartphone, turn on the TV, or reach for something to eat, smoke, or drink. We do not allow the comfort food of pure fantasy or wishful thinking to take us elsewhere. We abide in full awareness with no agenda. From this place, and this place only, something new, something unrestrained by our previous concepts, wishes, and expectations, can be recognized as happening.

This apprehending of the whole is itself the experience of the authentically new. In fact, the world is always new, always changing. Our problem is that our conditioning, often fear-based, applies a filter to this new world. The filter applies our current mental models (the way we make sense and keep ourselves supposedly safe in the face of all this change) to what is actually new, actually occurring for the first (and last) time. That is why we experience such resistance (distracting thoughts and emotions, dozens of reasons to stop the practice and get up and do something) to the practice of free attention, or to any other authentic meditation practice (as opposed to those that are focused on self-calming, which only enhances the filtering and selecting process). We have learned to attend to a selective version of reality. In doing so, we may become more efficient for short periods of time but we do so at the price of a deadening to the fullness of ever-new life in its intricacy and power. When we persist in the practice of free attention, more and more we gain a sense of what we have been missing.

We also begin to see that, wonderfully, the intelligence that can experience the whole, that can experience the new, can be cultivated. The practice of free attention is complete in itself and, by taking no further step but continuing diligently, we can continue to gain freedom from the hold of our conditioning. This is the goal of many of the meditation practices that have found their way into the wider culture in the past thirty or forty years.

But there is a problem if we stop here. With free attention we can experience the truly new, but we cannot have it, we cannot use it, we cannot know in just what way our world is different. That is because the implicit knowing of free attention is pre-symbolic, pre-language. We need language, new language, in order to pick up and use new experience. If our task is to be alert to what about our now needs, and be able to truly *act* in response, then we must take two more steps. The first is to learn a way to focus on that particular place, still before language, where the new world offers us the very beginnings of the language we will need to fully know it. This focusing (a practice originated by Eugene Gendlin) is the second step in the cultivation that each of the four fields require.

Implicit Intelligence

Step Two: The Unclear Edge

(Recognizing the Necessary New)

The open field of free attention is not a blank field; something arises within it. This something that arises is what Eugene Gendlin referred to as the *felt sense*, "a bodily-felt unclear edge." When asked why you are *really* reading this book, you knew you had an answer and went looking for it, *in your body*. You "had" an answer to why you are really reading this book, but it was a feel in the middle of your body: a sense, not an emotion. It was as if you are standing in front of your door in the morning, ready to leave for work, but you realize that you have forgotten something. You know you were supposed to bring . . . You made a note of it when you first woke in the morning, but right now it escapes you. You then do what human beings do, you stand motionless and look for the place in you that does know, that does remember. Most of us focus somewhere deep in our torso for that feel, felt sense, of what it is. It is right there, you have a feel for it, but it seems just out of reach. You stay with that feel of it, persisting, what is it, what is it . . . oh, of course, you need to return the book you borrowed from your colleague that you have been feeling guilty about for months now. Immediately the gnawing felt sense disperses and you carry forward your work-going.

A felt sense is not an intuition. It is not decision-making by "gut feel." Intuitive decision-making is more like psychologist Daniel Kahneman's Type 1 thinking, a thinking that short-circuits the methodical, effortful, step-by-step cognitive effort of his Type 2 thinking. Kahneman has shown, in experiment after experiment, how this gut feel decision-making is both highly conditioned, and thus subject to bias, and prone to the use of short-cut "heuristics" that often miss vital ways in which the situation in front of us is different from the general case that we represent to ourselves through habit. The felt sense is almost the opposite of this. It is the direct apprehension of the full situation that we are sure that we do *not* know, and the choice and specific effort to stay with it with an open curious attention as it unfolds. The felt sense is *not* an emotion and, like trying to remember what was forgotten, it is *not* "getting in touch with feelings." It is, rather, a handle on the vast intricacy that you are at any given moment. How is it right now for you? First, establish yourself in free attention, then check and see (you may listen to me guiding you through this exercise here):

After stabilizing yourself for several minutes in the free attention practice, allow the sensation where your attention is resting to become a distinct bodily-felt unclear edge. Do not expect it to be anything in particular, just go to the edge of your attention as it is in the middle of your body, and abide there. How is it? What is it like? What is it like, this distinct bodily-felt unclear edge?

Allow this to emerge, allow it to be what it is. Your analytical mind might say, "What is going on here?" or, "Nothing is going on here!" Simply return your attention to that unclear edge and the sensation is forming right at the edge where your attention fills the middle of your body. Give this edge attention without any need to know.

Allow yourself to abide in this place where there is a "having" of your full experience without any analysis, without any need to pin it down. Allow it to develop, allow it to unfold, stay with it even if it seems as if nothing special is happening. Returning your attention again and again to the bodily-felt unclear edge is itself the very act of cultivating implicit intelligence. This abiding without knowing but with deliberate focused energy is allowing nothing to come between your awareness and how everything, each part of everything that is happening for you, works to affect each other part and be this intricate inter-affecting.

The felt sense might be in the pit of your stomach, it might be your solar plexus, it might be in your throat or somewhere in your chest. Stay with this bodily sensation as it emerges and shifts. It is your body knowing the whole of what your experience is, before you have any words for it. What is it like? Does it have a color? Does it have a shape? Perhaps a simple word or phrase or image arises that lets you know what it is like. Allow that phrase or word to arise but do not cling to it; keep your at-

tention on the felt sense as it forms and changes. Keep bringing your attention back. You are at a frontier.

Symbolic Intelligence: Finding New Language
(Keeping the Necessary New)

If we have a difficult experience, let us say a meeting where things did not go well in a big way, a lot is happening when we exit the room. There is a "churn" going on that has both a strong emotional element and a need to understand and perhaps to act. At this point, we have a choice. We can go onto our next task and get immersed in it as a comforting way of having a sense of competency and control. Or we might pick up our smartphone and get lost in the *New York Times* or a favorite blog. Or we could deliberately sit quietly and bring our attention to the churn and just sit with it, returning our attention again and again to just being with the felt sense of the whole situation as each new impulse for distraction and evasion presents itself.

The act of attention and the staying with the felt sense is the beginning of a knowing that is more than implicit, it is the beginning of truly knowing something new. At this point, there is a danger. We can lose what is genuinely new as soon as it forms. As a matter of fact, we do this most of the time. The flash of confronting the beauty of the constantly changing world, and noticing how it is changing us, evaporates as soon as it is formed. We do not fully "have" new experience until we have found genuinely new language that captures them. We must find new words. Not the old words generated by memory and conditioning, but fresh language that comes directly from the new experience. With new language, we can carry what is new with us, and use it as a guide to what needs to happen next. Human beings do not fully *know* until they have brought implicit intelligence into the realm of language. This finding of new language, this fully human way of knowing, is what I call *symbolic* intelligence.

The exercises in each of the four chapters of this book are designed to move the reader from a place of implicit knowing in free attention to the creation of new language. This process is the movement from implicit intelligence to symbolic intelligence. The sidebar is for each chapter giving Sophie Jensen's new language for her engagement with each of the Four Elements provide examples of this process.

APPENDIX II

A FREE ATTENTION EXERCISE

Sit in a chair with a comfortable but upright posture. Direct your attention to the middle of your torso, anywhere from your throat to your lower abdomen. Allow your free attention to rest there. Notice that keeping your attention requires an effort. As you try to do so, you become aware of the conditioned thoughts, memories, and images—and the emotions that come with them—spontaneously arising. This is not your "thinking"; it is mechanical and automatic. If, instead of returning your attention to the sensation in the middle of your body, you give attention to the stream of thoughts, feelings, and associations, they will become a storyline, and there will be a judgement: "This is good, this is bad, this is just neutral." You now have competition for your awareness and what you were doing with it.

Allow the emerging thoughts and emotions to follow their

own course but do not feed them with your attention, with your imagination, or with your will. Do not allow images to become a string of associations that in turn become a storyline. The trick is to see it happening and at that very point to redirect your attention to the sensation in the middle of your body. If you wish, you may return your attention to the palm of your right hand as your "foundation of mindfulness." For some people, returning their attention to the breath works best. Make a choice: center of the body, palm of the right hand, or breath, but once you make a choice, stick with it.

Have no expectations as you return your attention to your foundation of mindfulness (the middle of your body, the palm of your right hand, your breath). Allow your attention to rest there, giving your attention to the bodily sensation and the energy that it needs so as not to be caught up in the string of thoughts, emotions, associations, and judgements. Have an open and curious mind. Do not expect anything. Suspend the need of your analytical mind to figure out what is happening or to impose any type of order or understanding onto your experience. Suspend the need of your conditioned analytical mind to know, to have a sense of where things are going, or to have a sense of whether or not this whole endeavor is worth it.

This experience of free attention will be a threat, in fact, to that part of you that needs to know, that needs to pin things down, that needs to get somewhere. Continue to get nowhere, continue not to know. Continue to return your attention to your foundation of mindfulness. Continue to allow whatever needs to arrive to arrive. At first, it may seem as if nothing is happening, and your "inner critic" will tell you that this is exactly so and that you are wasting your time. Whenever the inner critic appears, a good strategy is to simply smile. Do not allow your inner critic or your judging mind to interfere with your open awareness anchored in your foundation of mindfulness. Simply come back, again and again, to your foundation of mindfulness in the body.

This practice of free attention is, in many ways, like pressing the "reset button" of our intention and awareness. When we rouse the intention and energy that implicit cognition requires of us, engage in the act of pure presence, and make the choice to remain in that process, we are allowing everything that is able to function in our life to function. We are allowing everything that needs to emerge, that wants to be lived, to emerge. We are leaving nothing out. Anything that has been exiled, because it was too painful, sad, angry or threatening in any other way, is now allowed to show itself. We do not engage in "short-circuiting" of our field of awareness through various addictions or subterfuges. We do not grab our smartphone, turn on the TV, or reach for something to eat, smoke, or drink. We do not allow the comfort food of pure fantasy or wishful thinking to take us elsewhere. We abide in full awareness with no agenda. From this place, and this place only, something new, something unrestrained by our previous concepts, wishes, and expectations, can be recognized as happening.

REFERENCES

The Work of Eugene Gendlin

My approach to implicit and symbolic intelligence is highly informed by the work of Eugene Gendlin. Although my use of the terms "implicit intelligence" and "symbolic intelligence" is not always the same as his use of similar terms, words, and ideas such as "focusing," "felt sense," "carrying forward," "thinking at the edge," and "implicit intricacy," as well as many others referred to in this book, originate in his work. Gendlin, a philosopher and psychologist at the University of Chicago for many years, produced an extraordinary body of work concerned with the way human beings experience the world and create meaning from that experience. At the heart of his endeavors is what he refers to as the *philosophy of the implicit.* His works vary in terms of intended audience and level of complexity. They range from his magnum opus, the extremely challenging *A Process Model,* to the readily accessible and practical *Focusing.*

Gendlin, E. (2017a). *A Process Model.* Evanston, IL: Northwestern University Press.

Gendlin, E. (2017b). *Saying what we mean: Implicit precision and the responsive order.* Evanston, IL: Northwestern University Press.

Gendlin, E. T. (1997). *Experiencing and the creation of mean-*

ing. Evanston, IL: Northwestern University Press.

Gendlin, E. T. (2007). *Focusing.* Random House Value Publishing.

Identity

Berger, P. L. (1984). *The social construction of reality: A treatise in the sociology of knowledge.* Harlow, England: Penguin Books.

Hendricks, M. (2018). Introduction to thinking at the edge. In *Saying What We Mean* (pp. 282–294). Northwestern University Press.

Scott, C. & Tucci, S. (Directors). (1996). *Big night.* [Film]. United States: Rusher Entertainment & Timpano Production.

Gladwell, M. (2009). *Outliers: The story of success.* Harlow, England: Penguin Books.

Community

Hofstede, G., & Hofstede, G. J. (2010). *Cultures and organizations: Software for the mind, third edition* (3rd ed.). Montigny-le-Bretonneux, France: McGraw-Hill.

Berry, W. (2003). *The art of the commonplace: The agrarian essays of Wendell berry* (N. Wirzba, Ed.). Counterpoint.

Necessity

Maslow, A. H. (1987). *Motivation and Personality* (3rd ed.; R. Frager & J. Fadiman, Eds.). Quarry Bay, Hong Kong: Longman Asia.

Horizon

de Chardin, P. T. (2008). *The phenomenon of man*. New York, NY: Harper Perennial.

Heidegger, M. (2008). *Basic Writings*. New York, NY: Harper Collins.

Jung, C. G. (1991). *The basic writings of C.G. Jung: Revised edition* (V. de Laszlo, Ed.; R. F. C. Hull, Trans.). Princeton, NJ: Princeton University Press.

Rahner, K. (1976). *Hearers of the word*. London, England: Darton, Longman & Todd.

Carrying Forward

Quote from Eihei Dogen's Genjo Koan

http://www.thezensite.com/ZenTeachings/Dogen_Teachings/GenjoKoan_Aitken.htm

Retrieved from The Zensite, 4/15/21.

Appendix

Kahneman, D. (2012). *Thinking, Fast and Slow*. Harlow, England: Penguin Books.